Ruth Naumann

Australia • Brazil • Japan • Korea • Mexico • Singapore • Spain • United Kingdom • United States

Tsunami
1st Edition
Ruth Naumann

Text and cover design: Book Design Ltd.
Typesetter: Book Design Ltd.
Production controller: Siew Han Ong

Any URLs contained in this publication were checked for currency during the production process. Note, however, that the publisher cannot vouch for the ongoing currency of URLs.

Acknowledgements
Illustrations: page 20, 21 and 66 courtesy of Brenda Marshall.
Images: Cover image, pages 4, 5 (top and bottom, left and right), 6, 16, 26, 49, 59: courtesy of Shutterstock; page 5 (coastal erosion) courtesy of Auckland Regional Council; pages 5 (flood), 31 (sign), 72 courtesy of The Ministry of Civil Defence and Emergency Management; pages 10/11, 22, 31 (top), 34/35, 38 – 47, 54/55, 68 (top): courtesy of New Zealand Herald; page 13 courtesy of Matthew Hornbach; page 22 "Samoan tsunami?.. Really?", 4 October 2009, Tremain, Garrick courtesy of Alexander Turnbull Library; page 28 courtesy of World Vision New Zealand; pages 28/29 (background image), 33 courtesy of NASA; pages 36/37,52/53 courtesy of New Zealand Defence Force; page 57 Kiwi - a flightless bird from New Zealand; heads immediately for the beach during a tsunami warning, 2 October 2009, Winter courtesy of Alexander Turnbull Library; page 58 "Was that it?" 'Tsunami alert - Beach closed', 1 October 2009 Nisbet, Alistair courtesy of Alexander Turnbull Library; page 61 (left) courtesy of Tairawhiti Museum; page 61 (middle) courtesy of Whakatane Museum & Gallery; page 61 (right), Fish stranded by a tsunami, Harold J Dunstan, March 1947, courtesy of Alexander Turnbull Library; pages 62/63 (all) courtesy of NOAA; page 68 (bottom) courtesy of Pacific Tsunami Museum; page 69 'In loving memory', 2 October 2009, Scott, Thomas; courtesy of Alexander Turnbull Library; page 73 courtesy of NIWA.

For product information and technology assistance,
in Australia call **1300 790 853**;
in New Zealand call **0800 449 725**

For permission to use material from this text or product, please email **aust.permissions@cengage.com**

National Library of New Zealand Cataloguing-in-Publication Data
Naumann, Ruth.
Tsunami : case study of an extreme natural event / Ruth Naumann.
ISBN 978-0170189-44-6
1. Tsunamis—Case studies—Juvenile literature. [1. Tsunamis.
2. Natural disasters. 3. Ocean waves.] I. Title.
551.4637—dc 22

Cengage Learning Australia
Level 7, 80 Dorcas Street
South Melbourne, Victoria Australia 3205

Cengage Learning New Zealand
Unit 4B Rosedale Office Park
331 Rosedale Road, Albany, North Shore 0632, NZ

For learning solutions, visit **cengage.com.au**

Printed in China by China Translation & Printing Services.
1 2 3 4 5 6 7 14 13 12 11 10

ISBN 9780170189446

Contents

1 What is an Extreme Natural Event?

extreme = far-from-ordinary

For example, extreme sport is also called action sport and adventure sport. It is sport such as freestyle skiing and base jumping. They involve amazing stunts and adrenaline rushes. They are far-from-ordinary sports because they are about people taking the ordinary sports of skiing and parachuting to the edge. [Base as in base jumping stands for the four things people can jump from – buildings, antennae, spans (bridges) and earth (cliffs).]

natural = to do with nature

Nature is the environment that is NOT created by people. It includes things like rivers and rainbows, seas and storms, valleys and vultures, landslides and lizards, monkeys and mountains.

event = something that happens

Lightning hitting the tree under which someone is sheltering is an event. A ski race is an event. A rock concert is an event. A flood is an event.

Therefore

An extreme natural event = a far-from-ordinary happening caused by nature.

 ISBN 9780170189446

When a natural event becomes extreme

A natural event becomes extreme because of its **BIG SIZE** (size = its magnitude) and/or its **BIG LENGTH OF TIME** (length of time = its duration).	**size/length of time**		**extreme natural event**
	BIG water rise	=	flood
	BIG slide of land	=	landslide
	BIG snow storm	=	blizzard
	BIG wave	=	tsunami
	LONG dry spell	=	drought
	BIG explosion	=	volcanic eruption
	BIG ground movement	=	earthquake
	BIG/LONG wildfire	=	bushfire
	BIG thunder and lightning	=	thunderstorm
	BIG hailstones	=	hailstorm
	BIG slide of snow and ice	=	avalanche
	LONG-term wearing away of land	=	coastal erosion
	BIG storm, BIG rains, BIG winds	=	tropical cyclone (hurricane, typhoon)

Where the extreme natural event *starts* (originates)

Climatic events originate above the surface of Earth.

Surface events originate on the surface of Earth.

Tectonic events originate inside Earth.

tectonic = word from the Greek 'tekton', meaning builder; is about how events build the Earth

The difference between *might damage* and *does damage*

When an extreme natural event might damage people or property, it is called a natural hazard.

hazard = possible cause of great damage

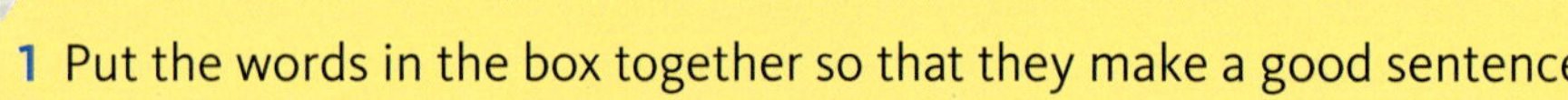

1 Put the words in the box together so that they make a good sentence.

happening	natural	nature	far-from-ordinary
by a	an is	extreme	caused event

2 List in alphabetical order 12 types of extreme natural events. Tick the ones you have experienced or seen on TV or in a movie.

3 You will be studying a tsunami that hit Samoa in 2009. Why was the tsunami called an extreme natural event?

4 Fix the spelling mistakes in the following: techtonic, climmatic, vulcanic, naturel, enviroment, tsunnami, durashion, magnetude.

5 Explain the difference between a hazard and a disaster.

6 Draw a labelled illustration to show the three places that extreme natural events can originate.

7 List the extreme natural events from the following New Zealand disasters:

1846 Taupo landslide kills 60
1863 HMS Orpheus shipwreck kills 189
1896 Brunner mine accident kills 65
1938 Kopuawhara flood kills 21
1953 Tangiwai railway accident kills 151
1968 Inangahua earthquake kills 3
1855 Wairarapa earthquake kills 5-9
1886 Mount Tarawera eruption kills about 120
1931 Napier earthquake kills about 256
1947 Ballantyne Department Store's fire kills 41
1968 *Wahine* shipwreck kills 51
1979 Mount Erebus aircrash kills 257

 ISBN 9780170189446

2 What is a Tsunami?

A tsunami is ...

- said as SOO NAH MEE.
- the Japanese word for 'harbour wave' (tsu = harbour, nami = wave).
- not a tidal wave or a 'normal' wave.

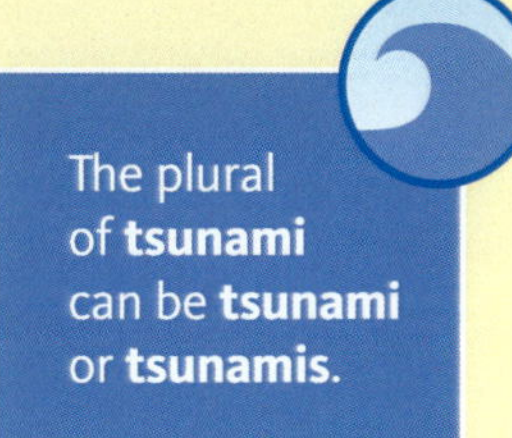

The plural of **tsunami** can be **tsunami** or **tsunamis**.

Difference between normal waves and tsunamis

Normal waves come and go without flooding the land.

Normal waves involve motion only at the top layer of the water. Therefore a normal wave is like a ripple on the ocean surface.

Tsunamis race over land as walls of water.

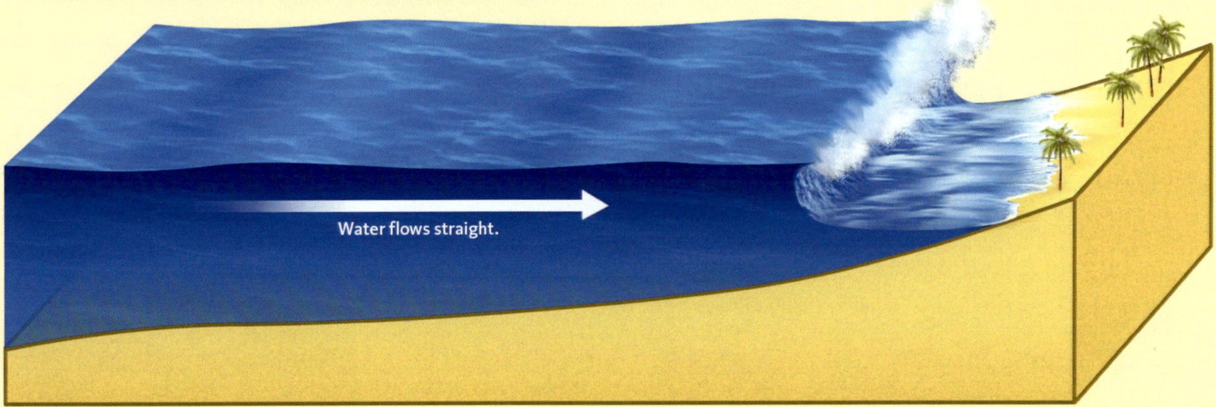

Tsunami waves involve movement of the whole water column from the ocean floor to the surface. Therefore tsunamis are like the whole ocean getting deeper all at once.

The tsunami processes

Processes are actions that shape environments.

1 Movement in Earth's crust (its outer layer) sends shock waves outwards. The movement could be

- an underwater earthquake
- a coastal earthquake
- a big underwater volcanic eruption
- an underwater landslide
- a big landslide from cliffs on the coast or a lake
- an asteroid/meteor impact with the ocean.

2 A column of water from the sea's floor to the surface forms. On the surface it has a wave-crest and a wave-trough. Tsunami waves in deep water are generally less than a metre high on the water surface. Big ships and planes don't notice them although new satellites with special technology can pick up big tsunamis in deep ocean.

3 Within minutes of the earthquake the tsunami waves split into two. One travels towards the nearby coast. It is called a local tsunami. One travels out to deep ocean. It may hit a coast many hours later. It is called a distant tsunami. The tsunami that hit Samoa was a local tsunami. Waves can travel crest-first or trough-first. Waves travel in ever-widening circles. They can travel at speeds of up to 800 to 1,000 kms an hour and be hundreds of kms long. They can cross oceans and yet when they hit land still have some of their original energy.

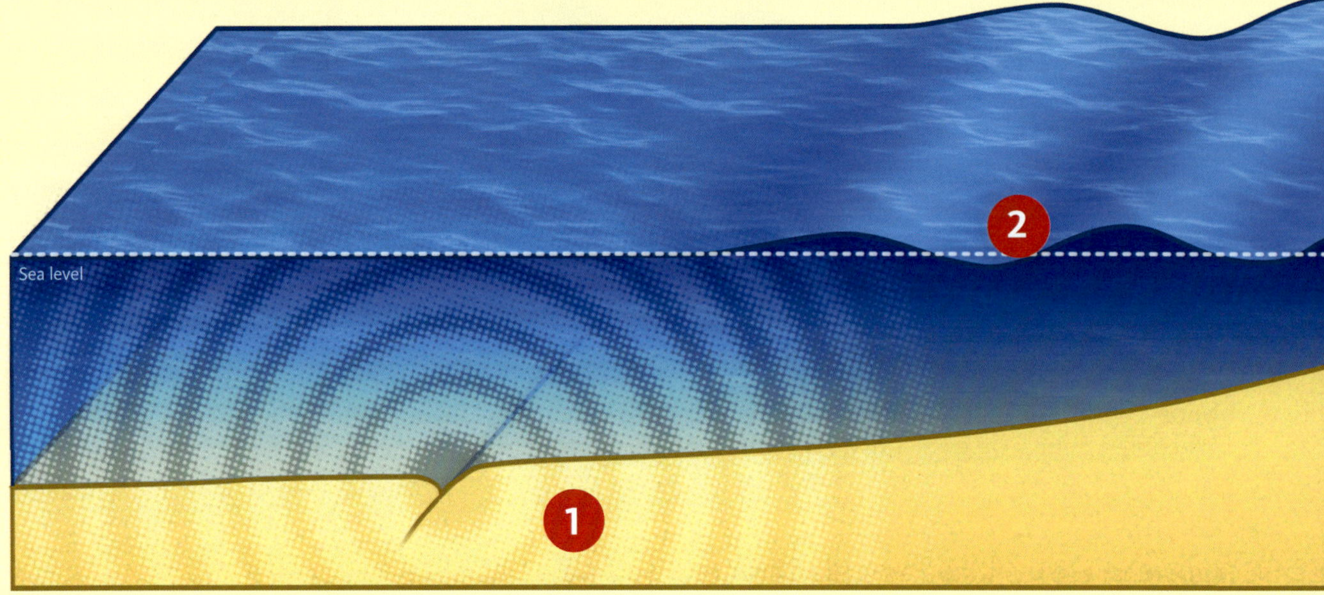

Warning signs of a possible tsunami

- an earthquake
- the ocean receding unusually and quickly
- gas bubbling to the water surface
- a smell of rotten eggs in the water
- water stinging the skin
- a noise such as roaring or booming
- a flash of red light near the horizon
- the top of the approaching wave glowing red.

Samoans call a tsunami **'galuafi'** – a wave of fire – to show its link with volcanic eruptions and earthquakes.

The French call it **'raz de marée'** – the violent rising of the sea.

Germans call it **'flutwelle'** – flood wave.

 ISBN 9780170189446

4 In shallower water near the coast waves slow down. They can grow to heights of 15 metres or more. Sometimes the ocean draws down and sucks water away from the coast. The water is said to recede – to pull back. It recedes so much it exposes the ocean floor.

5 Minutes later, the wave hits. Tonnes of water push it forward. So instead of breaking on the shore the wave continues to move onwards. Some tsunamis are walls of churning and foaming water. Others are fast-rising or falling water levels. Both types travel across land faster than you can run. The backwash (backwards flow of water) from a retreating tsunami can do as much damage as the surge forward. When a backwash bangs into a forward surge, the water becomes a killing machine.

6 Several more waves may come. They may be minutes or hours apart. Waves in distant-source tsunamis spread out across the ocean and lose some energy. But when they move on to a continental shelf – the underwater shelf that surrounds a land mass – they can grow in height because the water is shallower. When the waves reach harbours and parts of the coast that are more enclosed, such as New Zealand's Lyttelton Harbour and Whitianga, they can begin a sloshing movement. This slosh is known as a seiche. The word comes from a water expert in Switzerland. It means water swaying back and forth. The movement can build higher waves that can take a while to settle down. Tsunami waves can also 'bounce' backwards and forwards off headlands and underwater ridges and neighbouring countries. They might eventually join up to form higher waves in some locations. They can also grow in height because of friction effects from the seabed. This explains why the first wave is not always the highest. It also explains why waves can be small at one location and big at another location, no matter how close together the locations are.

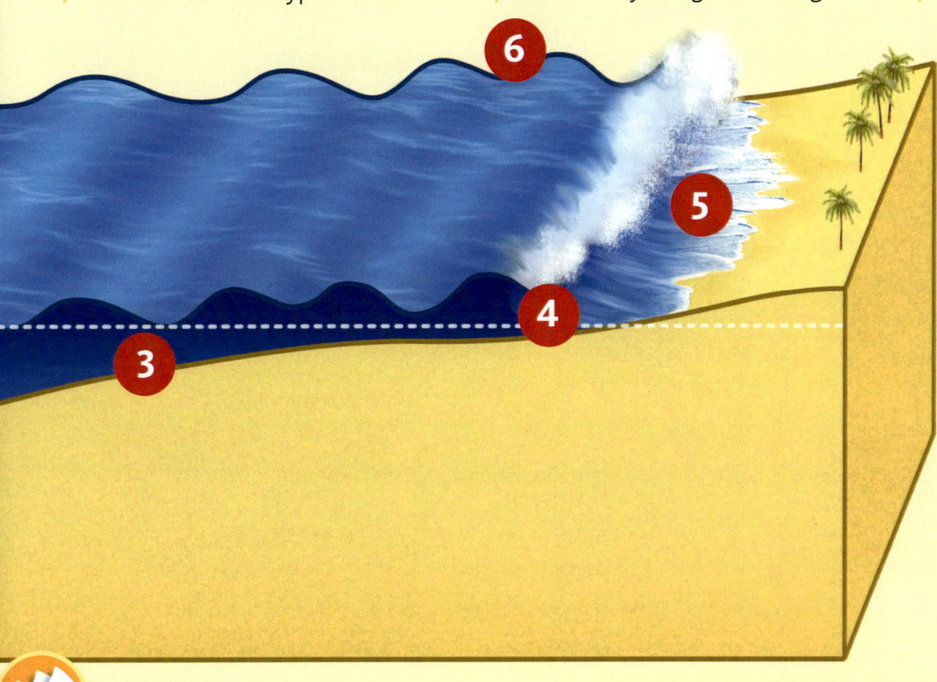

1 What is a process and why is the term linked with tsunamis?

2 Make a model to show how the height of a 14 metre tsunami compares to Tiger Woods (1.85 m), a giraffe (5.5 m), a kiwi (50 cm), a netball hoop (3.05 m).

3 What are the differences between a tsunami and an earthquake, between a local tsunami and a distant tsunami, between a trough and a crest, between a tsunami wave travelling in deep water and a tsunami wave travelling in shallow water, between a backwash and a forward surge?

4 What does 'recede' mean? Name two other things that can 'recede'.

5 If you were making a documentary about tsunami what music would you use for the soundtrack? Give some examples and say why you chose them.

3 Possible Effects of a Tsunami

Now

Effects can be immediate.
Eg. Two ways tsunamis kill people are drowning and smashing floating debris into them.

debris = the remains of anything destroyed eg. timber, tree branches

Later

Effects can be long-term.
Eg. People live with the fear that another tsunami might happen.

Effects of a tsunami depend on ...

- the size of the tsunami.
- how tsunami-aware people are.
- how far away a location is from the origin of the tsunami.
- the time of day when the tsunami hits.
- how long the tsunami event lasts for.
- how many people live in the location.
- what the location's buildings are like.
- what the location's vegetation is like.

effects = results, consequences, impacts of the event on people and the environment

 ISBN 9780170189446

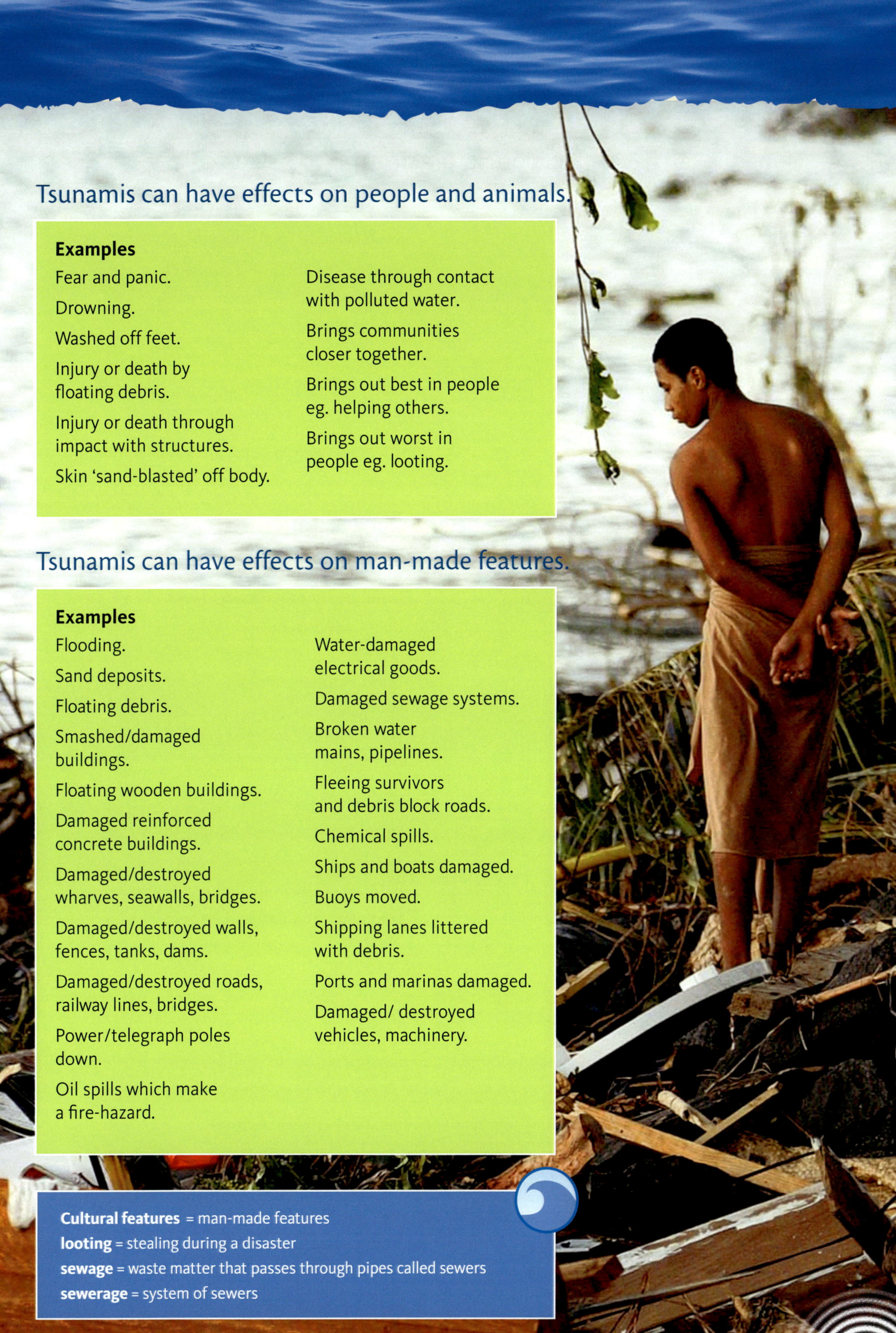

Tsunamis can have effects on people and animals.

Examples

Fear and panic.

Drowning.

Washed off feet.

Injury or death by floating debris.

Injury or death through impact with structures.

Skin 'sand-blasted' off body.

Disease through contact with polluted water.

Brings communities closer together.

Brings out best in people eg. helping others.

Brings out worst in people eg. looting.

Tsunamis can have effects on man-made features.

Examples

Flooding.

Sand deposits.

Floating debris.

Smashed/damaged buildings.

Floating wooden buildings.

Damaged reinforced concrete buildings.

Damaged/destroyed wharves, seawalls, bridges.

Damaged/destroyed walls, fences, tanks, dams.

Damaged/destroyed roads, railway lines, bridges.

Power/telegraph poles down.

Oil spills which make a fire-hazard.

Water-damaged electrical goods.

Damaged sewage systems.

Broken water mains, pipelines.

Fleeing survivors and debris block roads.

Chemical spills.

Ships and boats damaged.

Buoys moved.

Shipping lanes littered with debris.

Ports and marinas damaged.

Damaged/ destroyed vehicles, machinery.

Cultural features = man-made features
looting = stealing during a disaster
sewage = waste matter that passes through pipes called sewers
sewerage = system of sewers

Tsunamis can have effects on natural features.

Examples

Erosion of coast.

Erosion of sea-floor.

Flooded land.

Sand deposits.

Seawater pollution of land/water.

Trees broken or uprooted.

Cliffs gouged.

Salt pollution of land.

Reefs/sandbanks damaged.

Sewage pollution of land/water.

Fish and shellfish thrown ashore.

Drop in fish numbers.

Sand bubbling up.

Water tossed out of rivers and canals.

Waves on lakes and ponds.

Changed river courses and sea channels.

Tsunamis can have effects on social organisation.

Examples

International groups involved eg. Red Cross.

Government groups involved eg. Civil Defence.

Service groups involved eg. electricians.

Loss of schools means loss of education.

Specialist groups involved eg. search and rescue teams.

Police involved eg. keep people out of unsafe areas.

Medical groups involved eg. emergency hospitals.

Assessors assess damage.

Loss of leisure centres means loss of entertainment.

Insurance companies deal with claims.

Volunteer groups involved eg. collect aid money.

Loss of churches means loss of spiritual centres.

Local groups involved eg. clean up debris.

Counsellors offer support.

Businesses re-open or close.

New jobs eg. rebuilding.

Tourists stay away.

Disaster plans evaluated and revised.

Loss of equipment/buildings means loss of jobs.

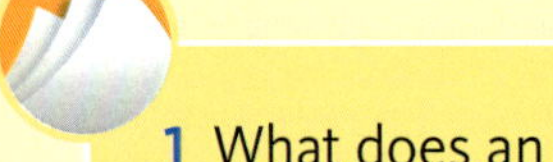

1 What does an 'effect' mean?

2 What do the effects of a tsunami depend on?

3 Why are the effects here described as 'possible' in the title of this unit?

4 Describe in words or a drawing how tsunamis can affect cultural features.

5 Describe in words or a drawing how tsunamis can effect natural features.

6 What actions do these people do? looter, assessor, evaluator, counsellor.

7 What is the difference between an international group and a government group?

8 Write a few sentences about the possible effects of a tsunami on humans.

9 Make and fill some speech/thought bubbles to suggest what the person in the photo (page 11) could be saying and/or thinking.

 ISBN 9780170189446

4 Tsunamis Around the World

What is the most important thing to know about tsunamis?

People sometimes think, during a tsunami warning for their country, that because the tsunami started a long way from them that by the time it reaches their country it will have faded away to nothing. Wrong thinking. Tsunamis can carry energy for long distances and a long time. The 1960 Chilean tsunami, for example, had enough energy to travel for 22 hours across thousands of kilometres to kill 142 people in Japan. The most important thing to know about tsunamis is that no matter how far away they start, they might still reach you.

What is the highest tsunami wave recorded?

On the night of 9 July 1958, an earthquake in Alaska sent rock crashing down into Lituya Bay in the Gulf of Alaska. The impact generated a tsunami. It was so strong it ripped away millions of trees and shrubs from as high as 524 metres above sea level.

Lituya Bay in the summer of 1958. Damage from the tsunami appears as the lighter-coloured areas on the shores where trees have been stripped away.

What is the biggest debris left by a tsunami?

Several hundred metres from the western coast of Tongatapu, Tonga's main island, are seven coral boulders. They are up to nine metres high and weigh up to 1.6 million kilograms. Scientists think they may be debris (remains) from a tsunami. They say the boulders did not form where they are now. They could not have rolled there either because the island is flat. They are made of the same reef material found offshore. The reef material is different to the island's volcanic soil. Satellite photos show a break in the reef opposite one of the biggest boulders. Some of the boulders' coral animals are upside down or sideways instead of toward the sun, as they are on the reef. Thirty kilometres west of the island is a chain of sunken volcanoes. Scientists think an underwater eruption or slide could have generated a big tsunami that swept the boulders ashore.

Note the size of the boulder in comparison to the people below it.

Why is Krakatoa so famous in tsunami history?

Krakatoa (Krakatau) is a small volcanic island in Indonesia. It slept until May 1883. Then it began to erupt. The eruptions climaxed at the end of August when one opened cracks in the volcano walls and let sea water in. This caused superheated steam to explode out and destroy most of the island. People in Australia heard the explosion. It is the loudest-ever recorded noise. The tsunami it generated reached heights of over 40 metres. It destroyed ships and rocked others as far away as South Africa. People panicked. A worker in a paddy field told how people clawing up a hill bit the heels of those above to try to make them shift up. Reports described skeletons floating across the Indian Ocean on rafts of volcanic pumice and arriving on the east coast of Africa up to a year after the eruption. The official death-toll was 36,000.

Is there a tsunami season?

No. And there is no average or normal tsunami either. Tsunamis can happen at any time, day or night, and anywhere.

What is the most destructive tsunami?

A huge undersea earthquake in the Indian Ocean on 26 December 2004 generated a tsunami. The waves damaged coastal areas in Indonesia, Sri Lanka, India, Thailand and other countries. They reached as far as Somalia on the east coast of Africa, 4,500 km away. Reports put the height from 2-3 metres at the African coast, to 10-15 metres at Sumatra. The tsunami destroyed the homes of millions and killed over 200,000 people.

Banda Aceh, Indonesia.

What is the earliest tsunami?

Scientists have found traces of a meteor strike from about 3.5 billion years ago. The impact on Earth would have generated a giant tsunami. Nobody knows where the meteor hit but the tsunami would have swept around the world in about 30 hours. Then it would have swept all the way back, met itself and swept back the other way again. Only mountains would have been safe. It would have wiped out nearly all life on land and on the surface of the water.

Earliest photo of a tsunami. The man died.

 ISBN 9780170189446

What are some big tsunamis from the past?

Time	Main Location	Cause	Deaths
365	Mediterranean	earthquake	50,000+
1692	Jamaica	earthquake	thousands
1707	Japan	earthquake	30,000
1755	Portugal	earthquake	10,000-60,000
1868	Chile	earthquake	thousands
1883	Indonesia	volcanic explosion	36,000
1896	Japan	earthquake	27,122
1908	Italy	earthquake	120,000
1923	Japan	earthquake	145,000
1933	Japan	earthquake	2,990
1946	Hawaii/Alaska	earthquake	165
1958	Alaska	earthquake/landslide	3
1960	Chile	earthquake	2,300
1964	Alaska	earthquake/landslide	130
1976	Philippines	earthquake	8,000
1979	Indonesia	volcano collapse	539
1979	France	undersea landslide	23
1992	Nicaragua	earthquake	170
1992	Indonesia	earthquake	1953
1993	Japan	earthquake	200+
1994	Indonesia	earthquake	223
1994	Philippines	earthquake	70
1996	Indonesia	earthquake	161
1998	Papua New Guinea	earthquake	3,000
2004	Indonesia/Thailand/Sri Lanka	earthquake	200,000+
2006	Indonesia	earthquake	668
2007	Solomon Islands	earthquake	52
2009	Samoa	earthquake	192
2010	Chile	earthquake	700+

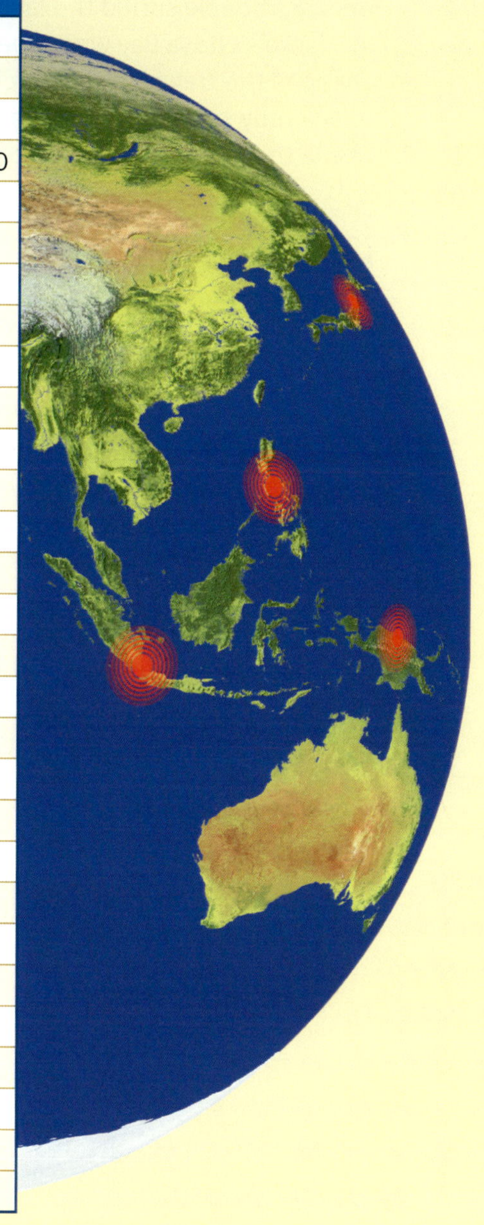

Can animals sense a tsunami coming?

Some people say yes. They say they have seen, before a tsunami, animals such as elephants and buffalo thundering off beaches to the top of hills, and animals in zoos hiding in their enclosures. Suggested reasons why animals sense a tsunami is about to hit, and humans do not, range from an animal sixth sense to animals picking up changes in Earth's electric field. Scientists have no proof of any of this. However, at an earthquake centre in China, videos watch snake farms across China. Earthquakes are often the first warning of a tsunami. The centre thinks snakes may sense an earthquake coming from 120 kms away and even five days before it happens. If snakes suddenly try to get out of their enclosures, even banging their heads against walls, the centre sends out an earthquake warning.

Has anyone surfed a tsunami?

Going out deliberately to surf a tsunami is one of the most stupid things anyone can do. However, in 1958 a couple surfed the largest recorded wave in history in a fishing boat. They were anchored in Alaska's Lituya Bay when the earthquake generated the giant landslide and tsunami. The tsunami snapped the trawler's anchor chain and tossed the boat up to the crest of the wave. Backwards and out to sea they surfed. Then the tsunami threw the boat stern-first into the ocean. Because air was trapped inside the hull, the boat floated bow-up. A ship later rescued the couple.

How is the legend of Atlantis linked with a tsunami?

Atlantis was described by Ancient Greeks as being an island in the Mediterranean. Legend says it sank into the ocean in a single day and night. Modern research suggests a giant tsunami destroyed civilisation on the Greek island of Crete about 1500 BC. Radiocarbon dating shows the tsunami could have hit Crete at the same time as an eruption of the Santorini volcano, 70 kilometres north of Crete. Scientists say the Santorini eruption was up to 10 times more powerful than the eruption of Krakatoa in 1883. It may have begun the legend of Atlantis.

1. With a partner or group, make a collection of the ten best pictures you can find of tsunamis. For each, give details such as location and date. Share with the class. With the class decide which is the best picture.
2. With a partner or group, gather evidence for or against animals being able to sense tsunamis before they arrive. Share with the class.
3. Like each member of your group, choose one of the big tsunamis from the past to research. Check that nobody else in your group has chosen it. Give a copy of your research to all members of your group.
4. With a partner or group, prepare a map to show countries that the 2004 Indian Ocean tsunami affected, and the approximate death tolls.
5. One of the most famous paintings in the world is Edvard Munch's 1893 painting called *The Scream*. Some people think its vivid red sky is the sky over Norway after the 1883 eruption of Krakatoa. Find a copy of this picture. With your partner or group, create an illustration called *The Tsunami*. Have a class vote to find the best illustration.

 ISBN 9780170189446

5 Where Samoa is Located

What is a case study?

case = event or subject

Eg. He is a hopeless case because he won't believe his girlfriend cheats on him even though she admits it.

Eg. The case of the missing leg puzzled detectives.

Eg. The tsunami made a good case for her study of how people respond to a disaster.

If you pick one particular extreme natural event to study in detail, you are doing a case study of it.

When you present a case study, such as the tsunami at Samoa, you need to describe the location of the case study.

Resource 1

Samoa and New Zealand are located in the South West Pacific Ocean.

The location of Samoa, and New Zealand, puts them in danger of several extreme natural events such as earthquake, tropical cyclone, and tsunami.

location = comes from a Latin word meaning 'to place' and 'location' means where a place is

resource = piece of information such as a cartoon, map or paragraph that is useful for your study of a topic.

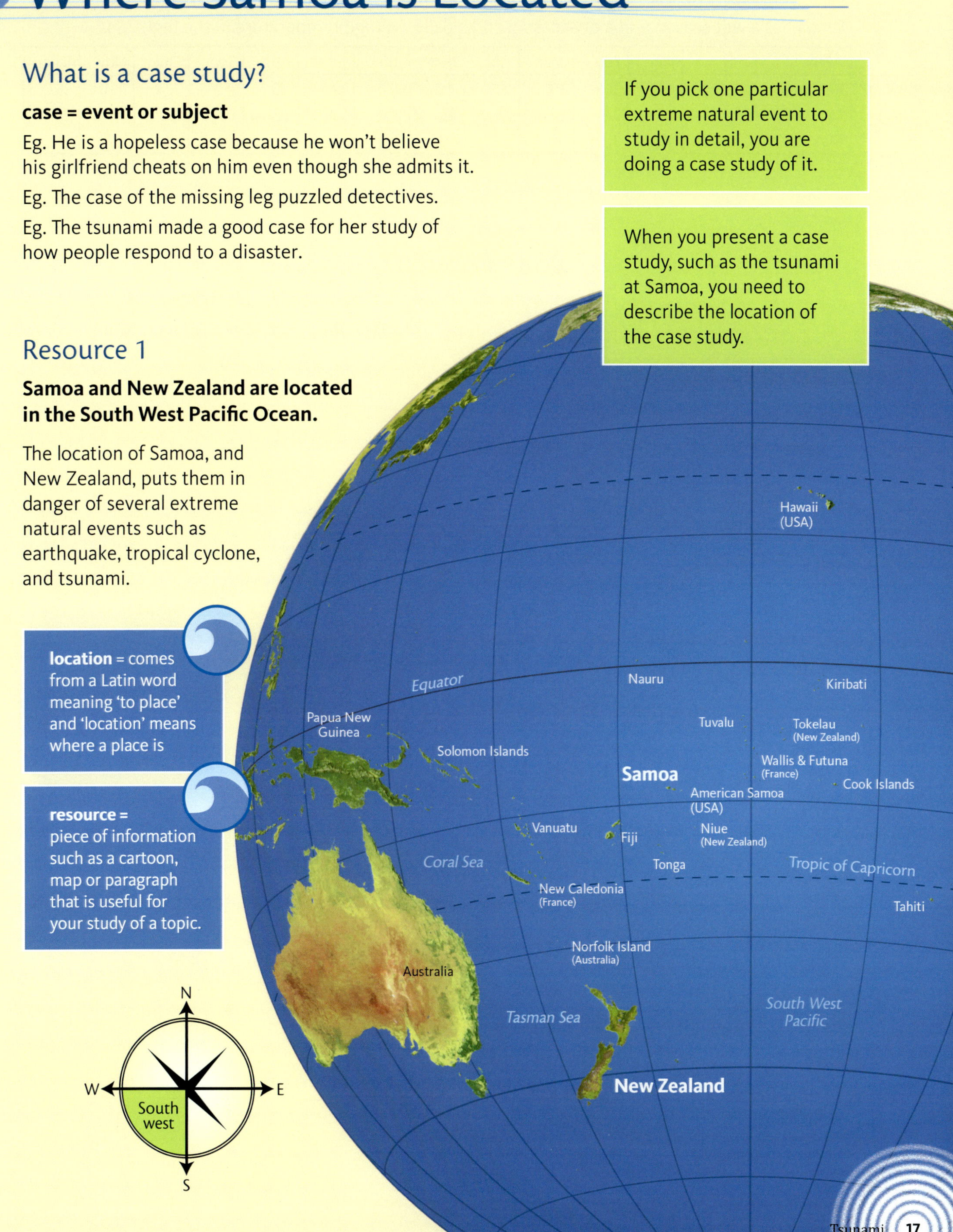

Resource 2

Samoa has a wet season and a dry season, and a daily average temperature in the high 20s.

APIA	Jan	Feb	Mar	Apr	May	Jun	Jul	Aug	Sep	Oct	Nov	Dec
Rain (mm)	489	368	352	211	192	120	120	113	153	224	261	357
Min Temp (°C)	24	24	24	24	23	23	22	22	23	23	23	24
Max Temp (°C)	30	30	30	30	30	29	29	29	30	30	30	30

Land area = 2,935 square km (New Zealand = 270,000 sq km)
Big town = Apia is the only one
Villages = several hundred; most people live in villages
Estimated population at time of 2009 tsunami = 220,000 (New Zealand's = 4.33 million)
Population density (number of people per sq. km) = low
Languages = Samoan and English
People = Samoan 92.6%, Europeans 0.4%, Euronesians 7%
Products = coconuts, bananas, taro, yams, coffee, cocoa, fish, nonu fruit
Big growth = industry eg. food processing, and Asian-owned businesses.

 ISBN 9780170189446

Resource 3

The International Date Line (IDL) is an imaginary (pretend) line. Map-makers put lines such as the IDL and the equator on maps of the Earth to help locate places. The IDL is where the date changes as you travel across it. In the Pacific Ocean it runs roughly down the middle although it detours so all of Kiribati is in the same half.

If you are travelling east when you cross the IDL you lose a day. If you are travelling west when you cross it you gain a day. This can be confusing. For example, to travel from Auckland to Samoa by air takes 4 to 5 hours. But during the flight you cross the IDL. This means you arrive the day before you left. New Zealand and Samoa have the same time but are one day apart.

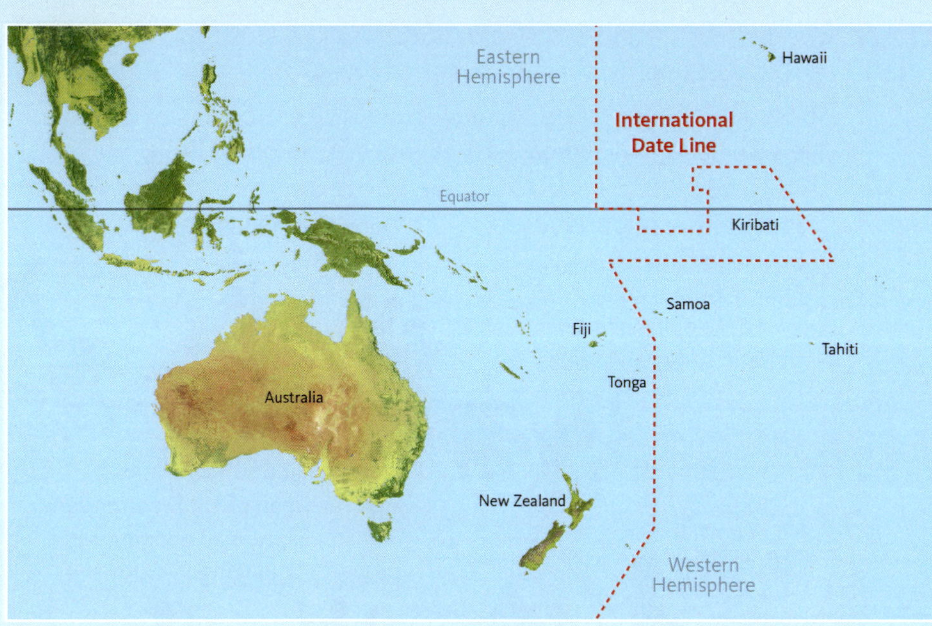

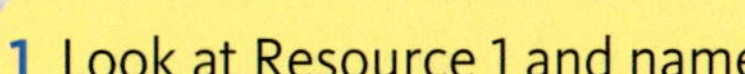

1 Look at Resource 1 and name
   - **a** the two Samoas
   - **b** the ocean in which Samoa and New Zealand are located
   - **c** two possible methods of getting to Samoa from New Zealand
   - **d** the country which rules American Samoa
   - **e** the country directly north of Samoa
   - **f** the two seas on the map
   - **g** the country which rules New Caledonia
   - **h** which country, out of New Zealand and Australia, is closest to Samoa.

2 Name from Resource 1, the two named and the one unnamed imaginary lines.

3 Look at Resource 2 and name
   - **a** the two main islands of Samoa
   - **b** the four islands that make up the Aleipata Islands of Samoa
   - **c** the capital of Samoa
   - **d** the feature shown by the shaded blue areas around the coast
   - **e** the word that means a strip of water between two pieces of land
   - **f** two small islands between the two big ones
   - **g** the two locations where you might expect to find ferries
   - **h** the highest point
   - **i** the wettest month
   - **j** the driest month
   - **k** what mm stands for.

4 What is a Euronesian most likely to be?

5 Make a graph to show the three major groups of the population.

6 Look at Resource 3 and name
   - **a** the word meaning 'half of the Earth'
   - **b** the hemisphere in which Samoa is located
   - **c** the hemisphere in which New Zealand is located
   - **d** which country, out of Samoa and New Zealand, is closest to the equator
   - **e** the hemisphere you would be in if you had travelled east and crossed the IDL.

6 Historical Links between Samoa and New Zealand

To understand the human response in New Zealand to the tsunami in Samoa it is necessary to know about the close links between New Zealand and Samoa. Past events are historical links.

historical = to do with the past

19th century (1800-1900)
Developed countries, such as France, Britain and the US, take over developing countries such as those in Africa and the Pacific.

December 1899

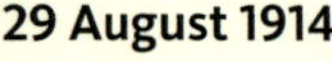

1914

WAR BREAKS OUT
Britain
Germany

1914

Dear little NZ, we want you to capture German Samoa from the Germans.
Yes, Mother Britain, right away.

29 August 1914
New Zealand soldiers land at Apia. German officials surrender. Soldiers capture all buildings and property belonging to Germans.

November 1918
Deadly and very contagious flu is killing people all around world. A New Zealand ship arrives at Apia with sick people. Ship had been quarantined (kept in isolation) in Fiji but sick people allowed to get off in Apia. Disease spreads fast. Kills about 22% of Samoan people.

1920
League of Nations (forerunner of today's United Nations) gives Western Samoa to New Zealand to look after. Nobody asks Samoans what they think.

1920s
Support grows for Mau ("opinion") movement in Samoa which is peaceful but determined to get rid of New Zealand rule.

28 December 1929
In Apia, New Zealand police and Mau marchers clash. 11 Samoans and 1 New Zealand policeman die.

BAM!

1962
New Zealand says Samoa (then called Western Samoa) can rule itself. New Zealand and W. Samoa sign a Treaty of Friendship to show they have a special relationship.

2002
New Zealand Prime Minister visits Samoa. She says sorry to Samoans for mistakes New Zealand made when it ruled Samoa.

2009
Tsunami hits. Samoa's worst-ever natural disaster. New Zealand gives immediate and long-term help.

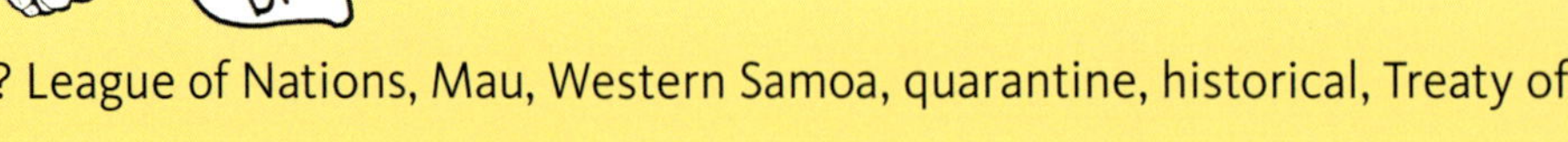

1. What are these? League of Nations, Mau, Western Samoa, quarantine, historical, Treaty of Friendship.
2. What is the difference between developed countries and developing countries, and what kind of relationship might they have had in the past?
3. Name six events that involved New Zealand and Samoa.
4. For each event, try to suggest a reason for the event, and a result of the event.
5. Why would Samoa in 2009 want and expect to get support from New Zealand?

 ISBN 9780170189446

7 Modern Links between Samoa and New Zealand

Modern links between Samoa and New Zealand meant that some Kiwis were having a holiday or visiting relatives in Samoa when the 2009 tsunami hit Samoa.

The last New Zealand census (count of number of people) showed well over 50,000 people who were born in Samoa live in New Zealand.	Many Samoan students come to New Zealand schools for education. 	New Zealand has Samoan superstars eg. discus thrower Beatrice Faumuina, boxer David Tua, former All Black captain Tana Umaga, entertainer Oscar Kightley, rapper Scribe.
There are many Samoan churches in New Zealand, especially in Auckland.	New Zealand tourists like to stay at Samoa's resorts on the beach in a fale – a small wooden hut with palm leaf roof built on log poles above the water.	Samoan cricket, kilikiti, is popular in New Zealand.
Samoans living in New Zealand send money home to their families in Samoa. 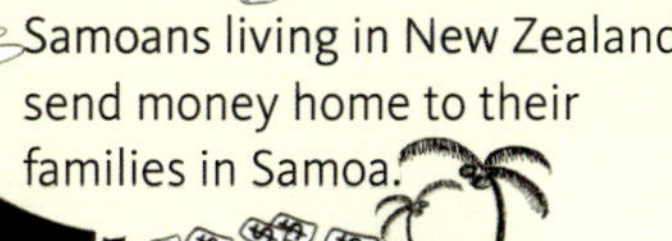	Both countries have a parliament and a Prime Minister. 	New Zealand and Samoan Government ministers visit each other. 
New Zealand gives millions of dollars in aid to Samoa each year. 	New Zealand sends goods such as timber, sheep and goat meat, bulldozers, and dairy products to Samoa.	Samoa sends goods such as phone cards, coconut cream, coconuts, brazil and cashew nuts and scrap metal to New Zealand.
New Zealand and Samoa play each other in sport eg. rugby, rugby sevens. 	Samoa can ask New Zealand for help eg. if another country invaded it. 	Samoa and New Zealand act as friends eg. recently New Zealand Army members planted over 300 native trees in Samoa after they spent 10 days training in the Samoan jungle.
Recently Samoa changed from cars driving on the right side of the road to cars driving on the left side. This means Samoans in New Zealand can ship cars with right-hand steering to relatives.	English is an official language of New Zealand and Samoa. 	Tins of corned beef from New Zealand are very popular in Samoa.
People in both countries share values such as the importance of religion and family (aiga in Samoa). FAMILY = WHANU = AIGA	Both countries are members of the Commonwealth of Nations which has a British Royal as its head.	Both countries are members of the Pacific Tsunami Warning Center. It is in Hawaii. It keeps watch for tsunamis. 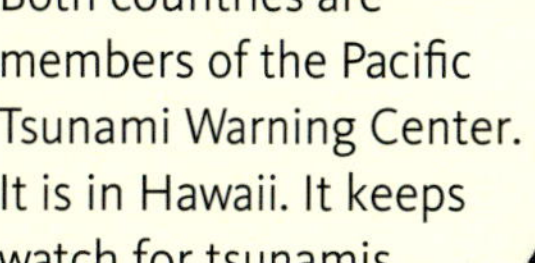

1 Give one piece of evidence to back up each of these facts.

a Samoa has an international port and airport.

b Samoans are the largest group of Pacific Islanders living in New Zealand.

c Samoans are very religious.

d Samoa and New Zealand trade with each other.

e New Zealand is Big Brother in the Samoa-New Zealand relationship.

2 What are aiga, kilikiti, census, fale, values?

3 In Samoa, everyone over 21 can vote. Only matais (chiefs), who are about 15 percent of the population, can be elected to parliament. What does this suggest about the role of matai in society? What role would you expect matai to play during and after an extreme natural event?

4 Write 10-20 lines explaining why and how Samoa and New Zealand have a special relationship.

5 Look at the cartoon and answer the questions about it.

a What is the name of the cartoonist?

b The boxer seeing stars is Shane Cameron. Who is the other boxer most likely to be?

c Give a reason for your answer to question b.

d What is the other boxer's relationship with Samoa and with New Zealand?

e Is the cartoon likely to have been published before, or after the Samoan tsunami? Give a reason for your answer.

6 Find out how kilikiti is played.

 ISBN 9780170189446

8 Geographic Links between Samoa and New Zealand

Geographic links between Samoa and New Zealand mean they share a risk of some extreme natural events.

geographic = about Earth and its features

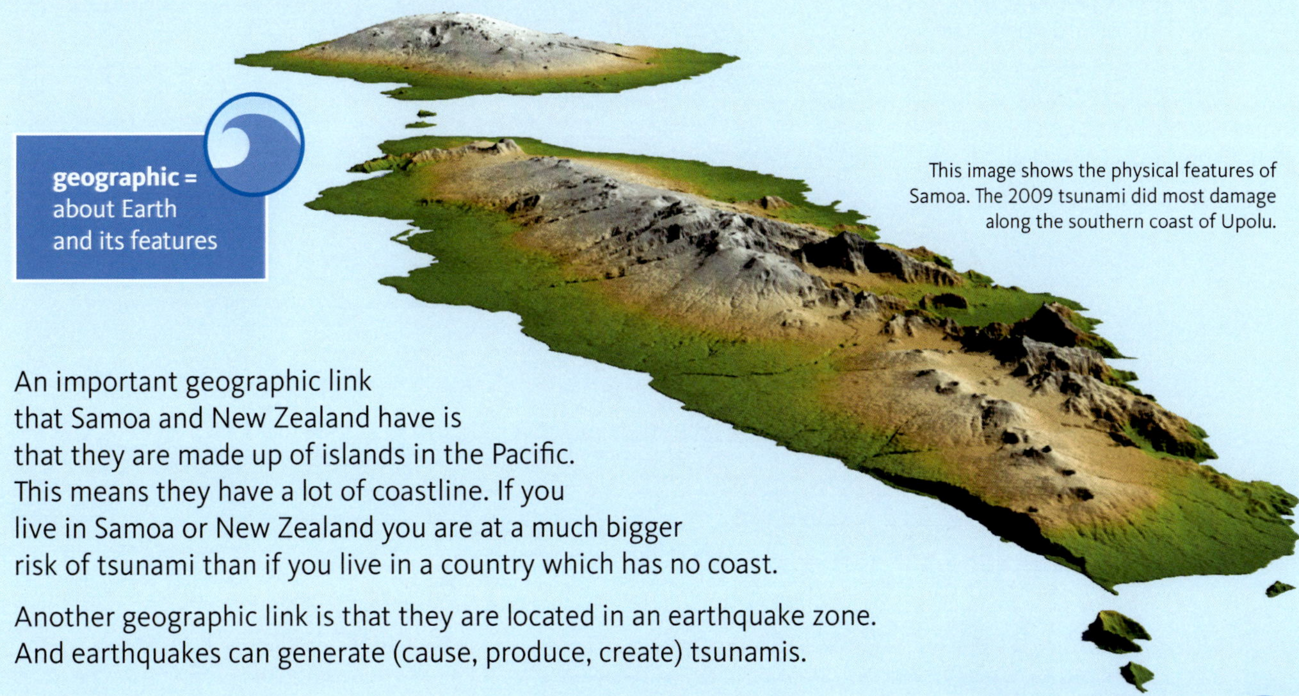

This image shows the physical features of Samoa. The 2009 tsunami did most damage along the southern coast of Upolu.

An important geographic link that Samoa and New Zealand have is that they are made up of islands in the Pacific. This means they have a lot of coastline. If you live in Samoa or New Zealand you are at a much bigger risk of tsunami than if you live in a country which has no coast.

Another geographic link is that they are located in an earthquake zone. And earthquakes can generate (cause, produce, create) tsunamis.

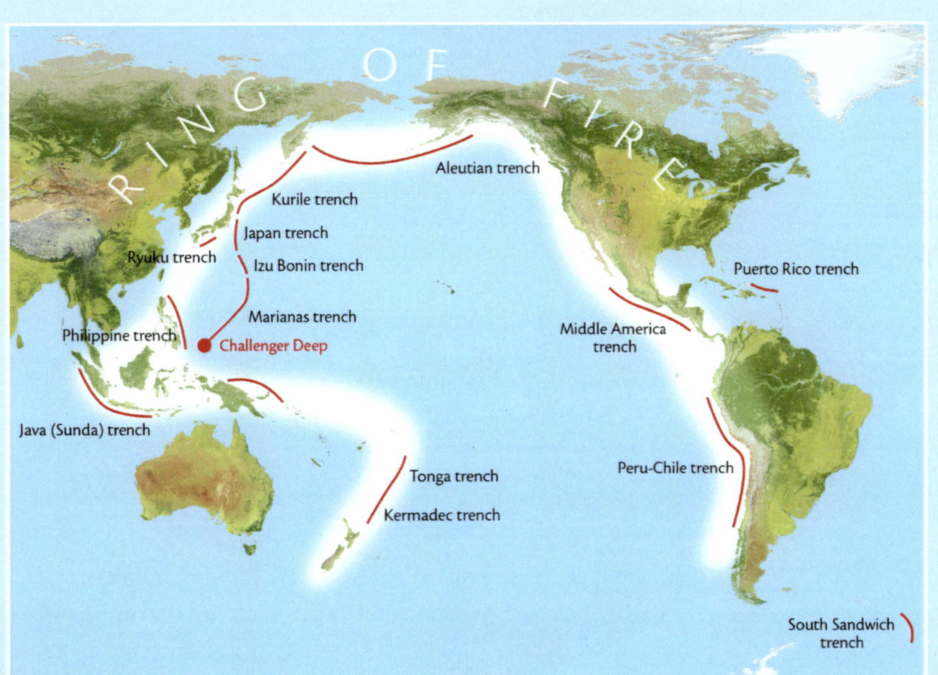

Ring of Fire = Pacific Ring of Fire; 40,000 km shaped more like a horseshoe than a ring; about 90 percent of Earth's earthquakes happen along it

trench = deep valley in ocean floor; deepest parts of ocean and lowest points on Earth; can go down about 10 km below sea level; can be thousands of kms long

Earth's outside surface is called its crust. Scientists say the crust is not one smooth covering, like the skin of an orange is all smooth. It is made up of about 30 plates called tectonic plates. So think of the crust as looking more like the skin of a pineapple.

Where plates meet each other is called a boundary. Most earthquakes happen around boundaries. This is where stress (strain) from plate movements is felt most.

The plates are slabs of rock. They are different sizes and shapes. They can be 5 km to 100 km thick.

In 2009 a break in the Pacific plate, as it went into a trench beneath the Indo-Australian plate, caused the big earthquake near Samoa.

 ISBN 9780170189446

Plates move a few centimetres a year. Sometimes movement causes a fault in Earth's crust at a boundary.

- Plates might move away from each other (called a normal fault).
- Plates might push together (called a reverse fault).
- Plates might slide past each other (called a strike-slip fault).

California

NORTH AMERICAN PLATE

This movement builds up stress energy in the rock at the edges of the plates. It might build up for thousands of years until the rock can't take any more. The rock on the fault breaks. This releases a huge amount of energy. This causes the Earth to shake — an earthquake.

Earthquakes hardly ever happen at the surface of the Earth. They happen below it, maybe even as deep as 720 kms.

Earthquake vibrations travel very fast, up to 14 kms per second.

The point on Earth's surface directly above the source of the earthquake is called the epicentre. This is where the shaking happens. 'Epi' means 'above'.

1 The science of earthquakes is called seismology. In Greek this means the 'study of shaking.' Is it a good choice of name or not? Give a reason for your answer.

2 Give five differences between your house and a tectonic plate.

3 Look at the Ring of Fire map (page 23) and answer the following.
  - **a** What is the shape of the Ring of Fire?
  - **b** Why is it called the Pacific Ring of Fire?
  - **c** What is the location of New Zealand on the Ring of Fire?
  - **d** What is the link between the Ring of Fire and earthquakes?
  - **e** What is a trench? Name two close to New Zealand.
  - **f** The map shows the deepest surveyed point on the planet. What is its most likely name?

4 Look at the Tectonic Plates map and answer the following.
  - **a** What are the names of the tectonic plates shown?
  - **b** On which plates is New Zealand located?
  - **c** Describe the location of the earthquake.
  - **d** What does the red dot stand for?
  - **e** The date shown for the earthquake was the date for New Zealand. What was the Samoan date and time of the earthquake?
  - **f** Describe where the Pacific Tsunami Warning Center in Hawaii is located in relation to where Samoa is located.

5 What is a fault? What three types of faults can happen at plate boundaries and what kind of movement is involved for each type?

6 Work with a partner or group to make a model or diagram of what causes an earthquake.

9 Earthquake near Samoa

6.48pm Tuesday 29 September 2009 (Samoan time and date)

Classification of earthquakes

Shallow	depths of less than 70 kms
Intermediate	depths of 70 – 300 kms
Deep	depths of over 300 kms

Shallow earthquakes often cause the most damage and increase the risk of tsunamis.

Location of the earthquake

- On the Pacific Ring of Fire.
- 205 km south of Apia, Samoa.
- 2,700 km northeast of Auckland, New Zealand.
- Depth of less than 70 kms.

Magnitude

- Is the measure of the size of the earthquake source and waves.
- Does not measure the earthquake's total energy.
- Is the same measurement at all locations eg. Samoa and New Zealand had the same magnitude.
- Is the largest wiggle on the seismogram.

Intensity

- Is the measure of the shaking and damage caused by the earthquake.
- Measures the effect of the earthquake on the surface of Earth.
- Changes from location to location eg. Samoa and New Zealand had different intensity.

Our earthquake words come from the Greek word for earthquake = seismos.

seismic = of or about earthquakes

seism = earthquake

seismology = study of earthquakes

seismologist = person who studies earthquakes

seismograph = instrument measuring Earth's movement during earthquake

seismometer = instrument measuring Earth's movement during earthquake

seismogram = graph showing Earth's movement during earthquake

seismic wave = shock wave that sudden release of energy sends out

Scales to measure earthquakes

The Mercalli Scale

- Is named after its Italian inventor – Mercalli.
- Measures the effect of the earthquake on the environment and people.
- Measures the earthquake intensity.
- Goes from I to XII (uses Roman numerals).

Mercalli Scale

I Instrumental	VII Very strong
II Feeble	VIII Destructive
III Slight	IX Ruinous
IV Moderate	X Disastrous
V Rather strong	XI Very disastrous
VI Strong	XII Catastrophic

instrumental = only seismograph, not people, notice it

 ISBN 9780170189446

The Richter Scale

- Was invented by an American called Charles Richter.
- Measures the magnitude of an earthquake.

Magnitude Classes

Class	*Magnitude*
Great	8 or more
Major	7 – 7.9
Strong	6 – 6.9
Moderate	5 – 5.9
Light	4 – 4.9
Minor	3 – 3.9

Each whole number on the Richter Scale is ten times larger than the number before it. A magnitude 5 earthquake has ten times the energy and ground movement of a magnitude 4 earthquake.

Scientists may change their magnitude measurements as they get more data in. This happened with the 2009 earthquake near Samoa.

Magnitude Scale

Magnitude	*Effect*
2.5 or less	Not often felt
2.5 – 5.4	Minor damage
5.5 – 6.0	Slight damage
6.1 – 6.9	Can cause much damage
7.0 – 7.9	Serious damage
8.0 or greater	Can completely destroy communities

Scientists say earthquakes probably can't get bigger than about 9.5. They say the only way to get more energy would be an asteroid crash.

asteroid =
solid object, smaller than a planet, orbiting a star

The Moment Magnitude Scale

- Was invented by a Japanese man called Kanamori.
- Measures the total energy released by the earthquake.
- Is the best one to measure major, but not minor, earthquakes.
- Each whole number is 31 times larger than the number before it.

1 Give five words, and their meanings, that come from the Greek word for earthquake.
2 What three different ways could scientists have measured the earthquake near Samoa?
3 What is the difference between magnitude and intensity?
4 Make up five questions that have 'earthquake' as the answer.
5 What words do the scales use to describe big earthquakes and their effects?
6 What words do the scales use to describe small earthquakes and their effects?
7 Show, by writing or diagram, the location of the earthquake near Samoa.

10 The Earthquake Generates a Tsunami

Samoa was lucky ...

Although people said the shaking seemed to last for several minutes, it did not cause massive death and destruction.

Samoa was unlucky too ...

The earthquake generated one of the deadliest possible effects – a tsunami.

Not all big undersea earthquakes generate tsunamis. However, the earthquake near Samoa:

- happened in fairly shallow sea.
- had a high magnitude.
- had movement violent enough to cause a sudden shift of a huge amount of water.
- was close to land.

These things together can cause tsunamis.

 ISBN 9780170189446

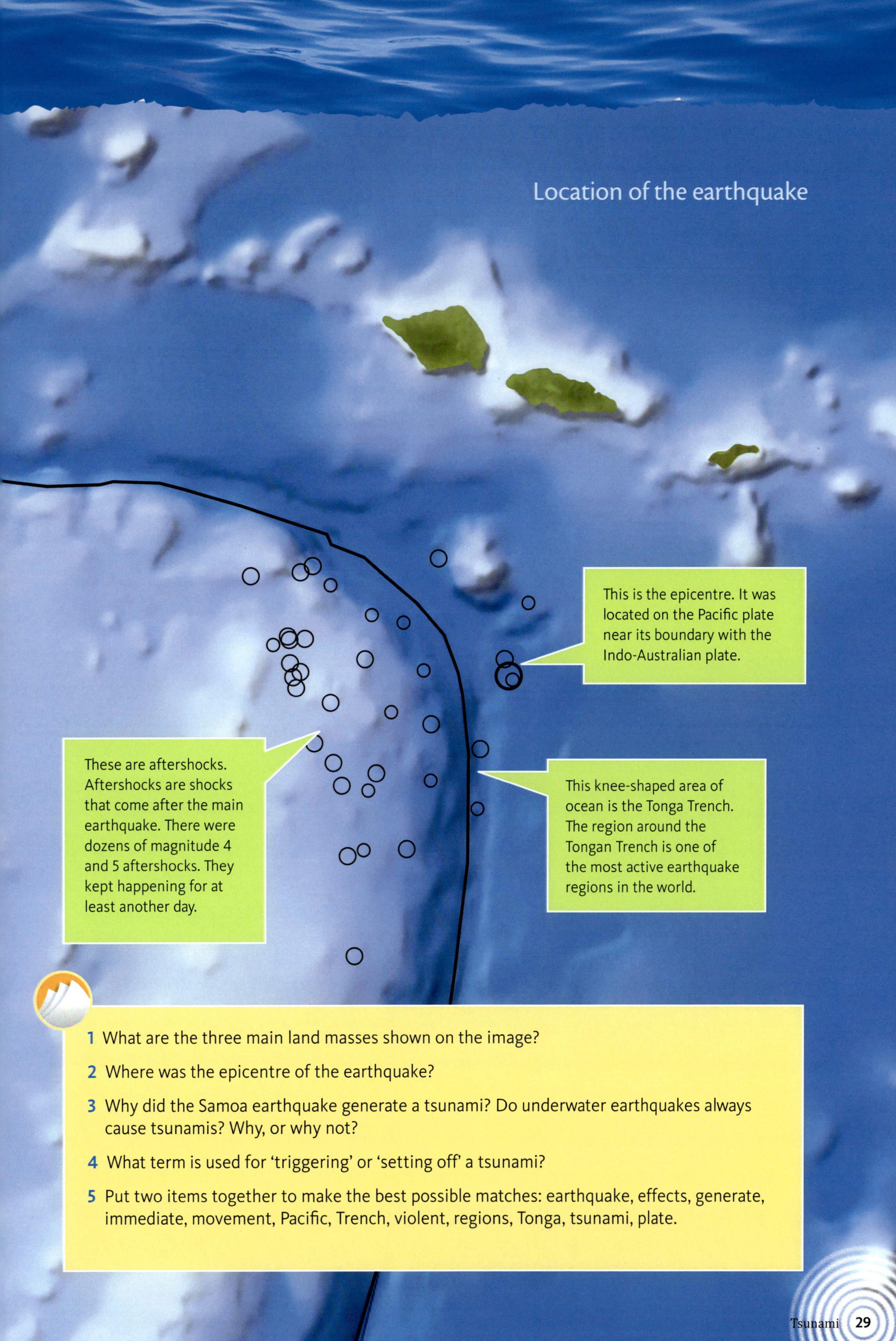

1 What are the three main land masses shown on the image?

2 Where was the epicentre of the earthquake?

3 Why did the Samoa earthquake generate a tsunami? Do underwater earthquakes always cause tsunamis? Why, or why not?

4 What term is used for 'triggering' or 'setting off' a tsunami?

5 Put two items together to make the best possible matches: earthquake, effects, generate, immediate, movement, Pacific, Trench, violent, regions, Tonga, tsunami, plate.

11 Two New Zealand Saviours

Receding water on a Sri Lankan beach, 2004.

Being able to recognise warning signs of a possible tsunami can save lives.

In 2004 an earthquake generated a tsunami in the Indian Ocean. The tsunami killed hundreds of thousands of people from many countries. Some tourists and locals walked around the seabed that had been left dry. They watched flapping fish and crabs. They wondered what had happened.

Then the tsunami roared in and killed them.

Some of the villages on Upolu's southern coast.

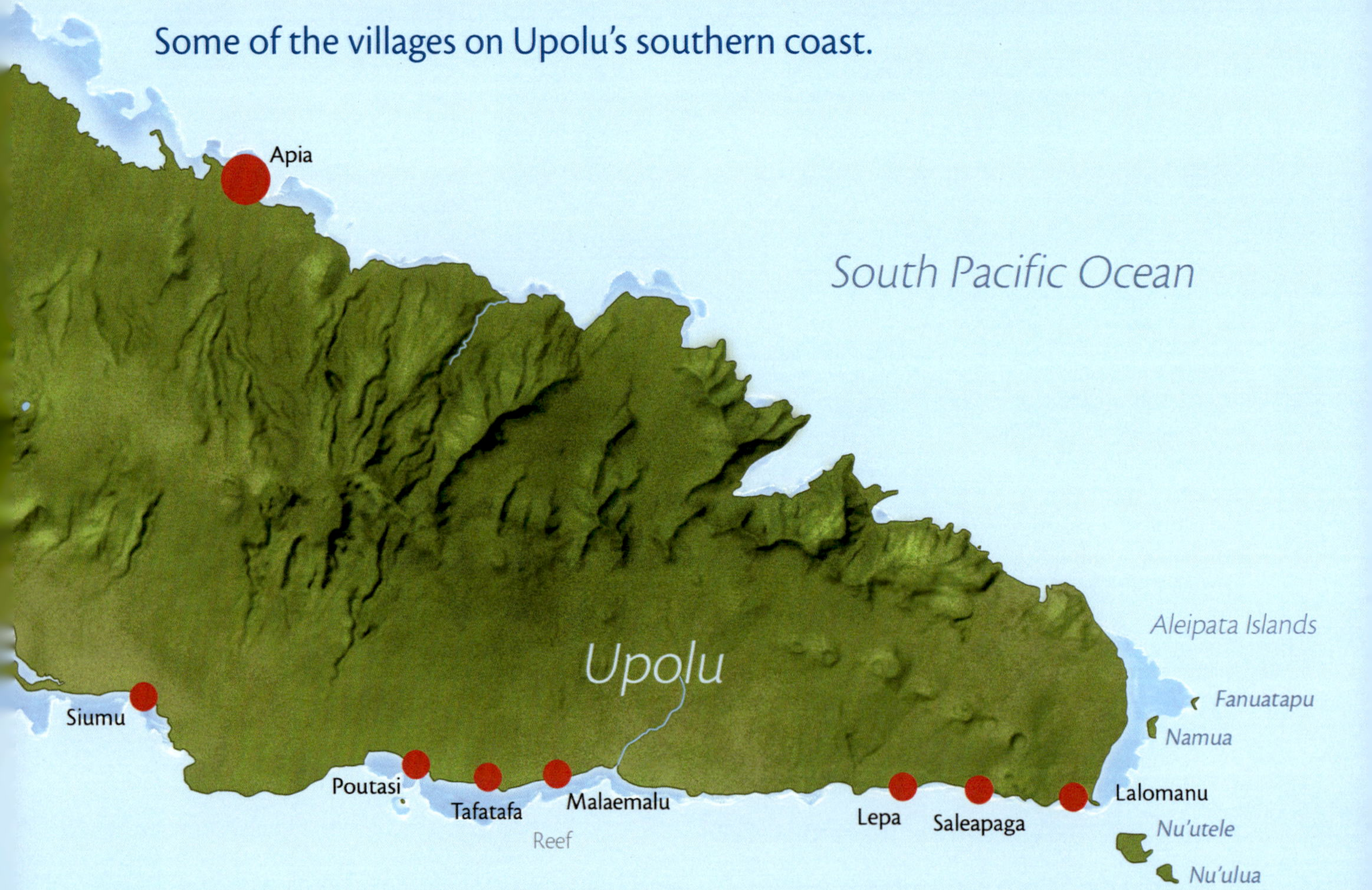

Apia
South Pacific Ocean
Upolu
Aleipata Islands
Fanuatapu
Namua
Siumu
Poutasi
Tafatafa
Malaemalu
Reef
Lepa
Saleapaga
Lalomanu
Nu'utele
Nu'ulua

At the time of the 2009 earthquake and tsunami, some New Zealanders were having a holiday in Samoa. A popular tourist resort was the Litia Sini Beach Resort at Lalomanu. It was about an hour's drive from Apia. It had beach fales for guests to stay in and the beach had coral lagoons (water between land and reef) for them to explore. Behind the fales were cliffs. In front were great views of Nu'utele Island. No people lived on the island but guests could visit and stay to learn how to survive using resources from nature.

 ISBN 9780170189446

Ten-year-old Abby Wutzler from Wellington was at the resort with her brother and parents. Also there with his family was twelve-year-old Maxwell Wilson from Albany. Abby saw the sea receding. She had studied natural disasters at school. 'Tsunami!' she yelled as she ran up and down the beach to warn people. She then raced for high ground. Maxwell felt the earthquake. Maybe a tsunami, he thought. Then he saw the sea receding. He yelled for everyone to run from their fales. He too raced for the cliff.

Abby and Maxwell did everything right. They warned others and ran for high ground. New Zealand Civil Defence presented certificates to Abby and Maxwell for their actions. The steep and curving cliffs of Lalomanu made a basin. Tsunami water crashed about in it for ten minutes before going. It dug into the cliffs up to heights of ten to 15 metres.

1 Describe what a saviour does.

2 Describe the location of Lalomanu. Include names of other places in your description.

3 What part of Samoa did the tsunami damage most?

4 If you had been Abby or Maxwell would you have acted differently? Give a reason for your answer.

5 Look at the New Zealand Civil Defence sign and answer the following questions.
   - a What does the word 'hazard' mean?
   - b What is the minimum height for the high ground that you should run to?
   - c What should you do if there is no high ground?
   - d What is the minimum time you should stay in your place of safety?
   - e Why should you stay away from rivers and creeks?

6 Draw and label the location of a lagoon. Include the reef, which is a ridge just under the surface of the water and at Lalomanu was made of coral.

7 Where could you find out if the resort survived the tsunami and how many people died at Lalomanu?

8 Design a certificate to award to people who help others before, during or after a tsunami.

12 Killer Waves

The tsunami killed 9 people at the Tongan island of Niuatoputapu, 149 people in Samoa, 34 people in American Samoa.

The tsunami at Samoa became killer waves because ...

Many tourist resorts were on the coast. Tourists liked the experience of staying in a fale and seeing the tide come in under it.

Samoan villages consist of land that runs from the coast to higher ground in the hills and mountains. Up in the hills are plantations such as coconuts and bananas. Many Samoans had houses on the shore.

The tsunami hit when people were busy with other things such as getting ready for work or school. Some children were already on their way to school.

The earthquake that generated the tsunami was so close to Samoa there was no time for the Pacific Tsunami Warning Center to send warnings to Samoans. The first alert from Hawaii was 18 minutes after the earthquake. The waves arrived six or seven minutes after the quake. It was up to locals to recognise the signs and respond. Some local alarms went off. In some places local men banged on gas cylinders to warn people. At some beach resorts staff noticed the ocean receding. They alerted guests, even breaking down doors to wake sleepers. They dragged guests out and sent them fleeing up hills. From there survivors saw the tsunami destroy their accomodation and wash away their belongings.

Tsunami surges roared ashore and swept inland for up to one and a half kilometres. Survivors said the waves seemed to reach the sky. Later, New Zealand scientists said they found three waves up to 14 metres high. The scientists measured watermarks on buildings and trees to help confirm the height of the waves. Wide reefs helped to reduce water height.

It was a local-source tsunami. This means it had less than one hour travel time to the nearest coast. Regional sources have one to three hours travel time. Distant sources have more than three hours travel time.

This was the worst natural disaster to hit Samoa since written records. The most recent had been a cyclone in 1990 which killed eight people and a cyclone in 1991 which killed eleven people.

 ISBN 9780170189446

Before and after the tsunami at Upolu island

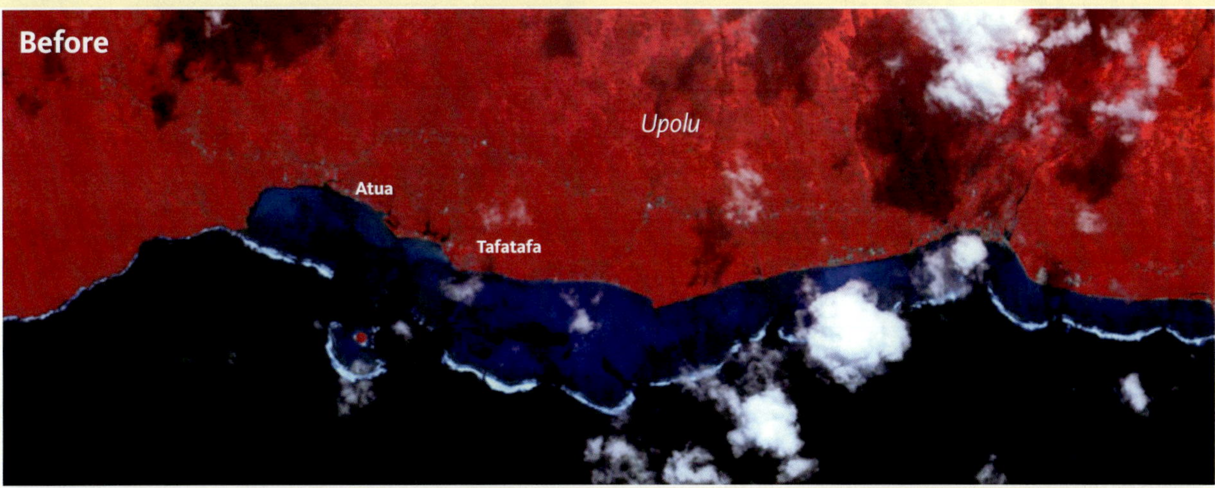

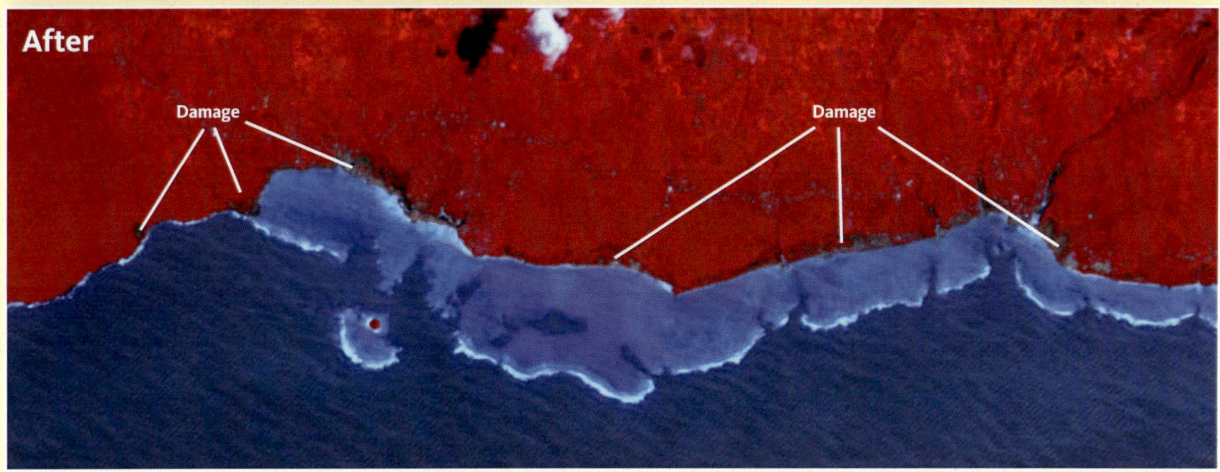

Although the tsunami did some damage to Savai'i and Manono, its main environmental impact was on Upolu. These satellite images show damage to vegetation (the red), and to the coast.

1 What was the total death toll from the tsunami?

2 Draw a labelled diagram to illustrate local, regional and distant-source tsunami.

3 Why was the tsunami called 'killer waves'?

4 Look at the two satellite images and answer the following.
   - **a** Why are there two images?
   - **b** Which island is shown and which coast of the island is shown?
   - **c** What does the blue colour stand for?
   - **d** Name two features that are white.
   - **e** The damaged areas of vegetation stretch about 300 m inland. There is also coastal erosion near Tafatafa. Explain the difference between these two types of environmental damage.

13 Immediate Response in Samoa to the Tsunami

A man held on to his wife. Water tore her free and drowned her. It churned him round and round underneath until he finally surfaced. Debris – bits of destroyed buildings, trees and vehicles – crashed into him. With his jaw broken, ribs cracked and legs and feet cut, he finally managed to cling on to a palm tree that was still standing.

A radio station worker watched from the office balcony as the tsunami struck. People down below screamed in fear. He yelled at them, 'Run up the hill!' But they ran down the street. Soon a river of mud swirled people, trees, cars, buses and boats past his balcony.

Some local boys dived into the churning water to get people. One boy rescued about five people.

A man staggered uphill with a woman on his back. They got to safety.

 ISBN 9780170189446

A Kiwi surfer felt the earthquake. He went out for a surf and joined other surfers from New Zealand. Suddenly the water went glassy and then bubbly. It moved them further out to sea. They saw how dry the reef was. They floated around in deep water until they could paddle back in.

Water swept people out to sea. Water swept people inland. It washed some in and out several times. As a car bobbed in the ocean its alarm blared.

People on a bus saw the first wave. They screamed, wept, tried to call home. Cell phones died. The driver put his foot down and the bus hurtled up a hill to safety.

A New Zealand couple on holiday were getting ready for a run when the earthquake hit. They saw the lagoon drain. They jumped into their car, let in another couple and drove towards higher ground. A wall of water raced over the top of the fales and smashed everything. It picked up the car and threw it across the road into a concrete toilet block. They tried to get out but the doors and windows would not open. The driver kicked at the windscreen until he made a hole. As water flooded the car they took last gasps of air. Everything went black. Finally there was a glimmer of light. Without knowing how, they got out and to higher ground.

The dogs of a local man gathered at the seaside after the earthquake. They barked and then fled to the taro plantations in the hills. He followed.

A four-year-old local was running from his house near the beach when the wave hit him. His mother and younger brother drowned. Tree branches pounded him but despite his damaged spinal cord and broken bones he hung on to a branch. The water swept him to an inland plantation of a neighbouring village. The water had also taken a cousin there. He heard the boy calling his father's name. He found him and carried him home. The boy's father was badly injured but alive.

 ISBN 9780170189446

Stunned survivors comforted each other while keeping a watch for further waves.

A New Zealand couple on holiday heard the roar of an approaching wall of water as they ran for the pathless hill. They had to jump a corrugated iron fence. The woman landed in a hole. The first wave reached her. It dumped two buildings on top of her.

A tourist clambered to the top of a water tank. She watched a wave pick up her husband. It dragged him through rocks and undergrowth and threw him into the jungle. He survived.

A British woman and her Samoan boyfriend thought the danger was over once the earthquake stopped shaking. 'Run!' yelled locals. The couple jumped into their car but five metres down the road the first wave cracked the windscreen and water poured in. He managed to smash a window and pull himself out. He grabbed her hand. Another surge hit. Down plunged the car. She lost her grip. Trapped in the sinking car, struggling for air, she panicked. Then she made herself relax and say a prayer. The back of the car rose out of the wave. She scrambled through the window. She found her boyfriend clinging to a tree. He had deep gashes to his back and torso. They struggled to higher ground.

ISBN 9780170189446

A mother saw the tsunami. She grabbed her baby son and young daughter. She turned her back to the water and braced herself. The water ripped her daughter away and drowned her. It killed six other family members and a visiting neighbour. For a long time she was under water. Suddenly she got air. She and the baby floated to the back of the village. She seized a coconut tree. In her arms the baby was lifeless. Praying, she sucked water from his nose. He coughed and came to life.

A chief and his wife who owned and operated a beach hotel were at morning prayers with a 95-year-old mother and her nurse. The earthquake shook the building. After prayers they saw the sea water receding from the lagoon. They got the old lady and her nurse into the pick-up truck. The wife jumped on to the truck tray. He drove fast for high ground. The wave caught them. It lifted the truck. When it stopped tumbling the chief's wife had gone. An hour later he found her hooked on branches of a tree. She was dead.

A villager was running from the tsunami when he realised his crippled father was still in the house. He charged back and had just thrown his father to higher ground when a wave dragged him out to sea. He ended up naked on some roofing iron. A second wave brought him back to shore. Although badly wounded he managed to get to dry ground.

Some people went to gather fish that the first wave washed up. The second wave hit them and they died.

An 84-year-old man was sitting in his waterfront fale when the earthquake shook it. His family begged him to follow them up the hill. But he could walk only with the help of a piece of wood and knew he would be too slow. Within minutes the wave hurled him up and away. He hit a power pole, a tree, a steel house post. He clung to the post. The sea ripped off his lavalava. Debris banged into him. After the waves went two of his sons came down the hill to look for him. They wrapped another lavalava around him. He had only a few cuts and bruises.

The earthquake woke a chief up. His son's family were in the cab of the truck getting ready to drive to school. He climbed on to the back. The wave caught the truck and rolled it around. The three adults survived. The three children died.

A young mother was playing with her three children when the earthquake rattled the house. She called her husband who had just left for work. 'Get out!' he said. She grabbed the baby. 'Run!' she told the other two youngsters. She saw the wave coming. She ran upstairs to the back of the house. The two children were running up to the mountain but the wave was too fast. It swallowed them. It crashed into the house and ripped it apart. It tore the baby from her arms. She hung on to a floating car door. For about 45 minutes water and debris threw her around. Then she was trapped between posts of a house roof. There she fainted. A man and woman found her and took her to hospital.

 ISBN 9780170189446

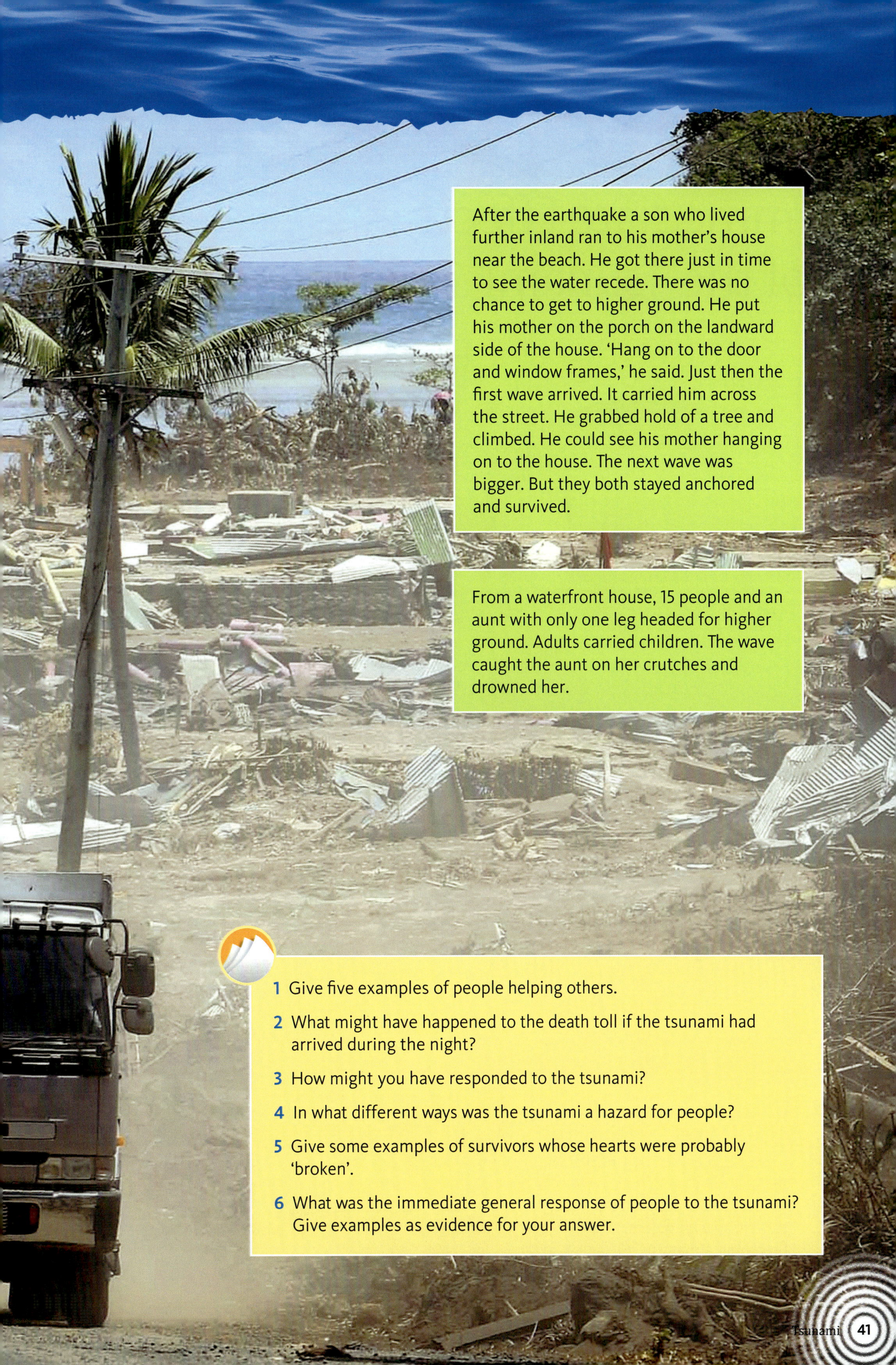

After the earthquake a son who lived further inland ran to his mother's house near the beach. He got there just in time to see the water recede. There was no chance to get to higher ground. He put his mother on the porch on the landward side of the house. 'Hang on to the door and window frames,' he said. Just then the first wave arrived. It carried him across the street. He grabbed hold of a tree and climbed. He could see his mother hanging on to the house. The next wave was bigger. But they both stayed anchored and survived.

From a waterfront house, 15 people and an aunt with only one leg headed for higher ground. Adults carried children. The wave caught the aunt on her crutches and drowned her.

1 Give five examples of people helping others.
2 What might have happened to the death toll if the tsunami had arrived during the night?
3 How might you have responded to the tsunami?
4 In what different ways was the tsunami a hazard for people?
5 Give some examples of survivors whose hearts were probably 'broken'.
6 What was the immediate general response of people to the tsunami? Give examples as evidence for your answer.

14 Immediate Effects of the Tsunami

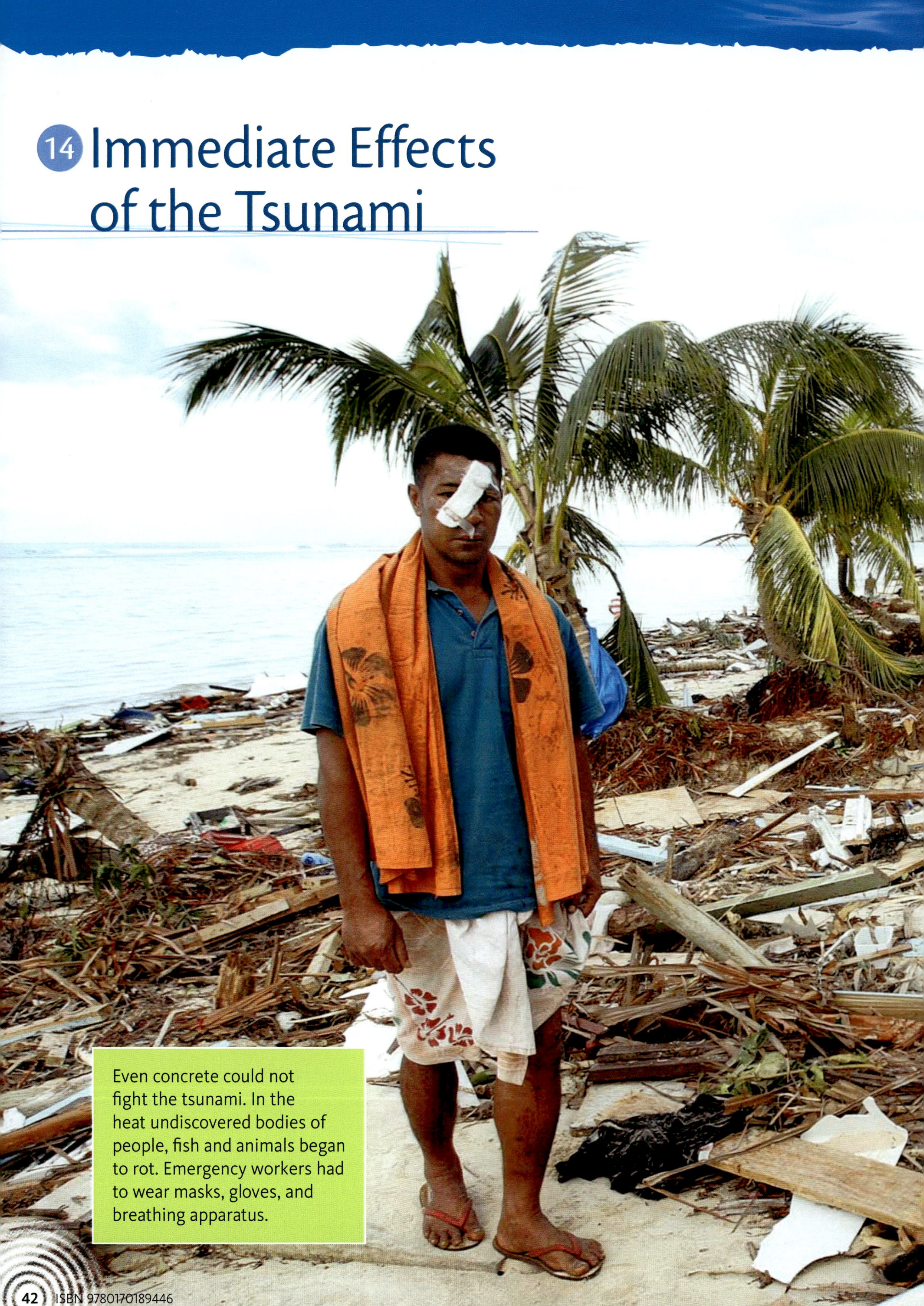

Even concrete could not fight the tsunami. In the heat undiscovered bodies of people, fish and animals began to rot. Emergency workers had to wear masks, gloves, and breathing apparatus.

 ISBN 9780170189446

Locals felt as though they were in a war-zone.

Villagers found cars in strange places.

The tsunami wiped out some villages. Silt covered everything for many metres inland. This villager is sitting where his home used to be.

Medics helped victims.

 ISBN 9780170189446

This boy needed something on his feet if he was to walk around what was left of his village.

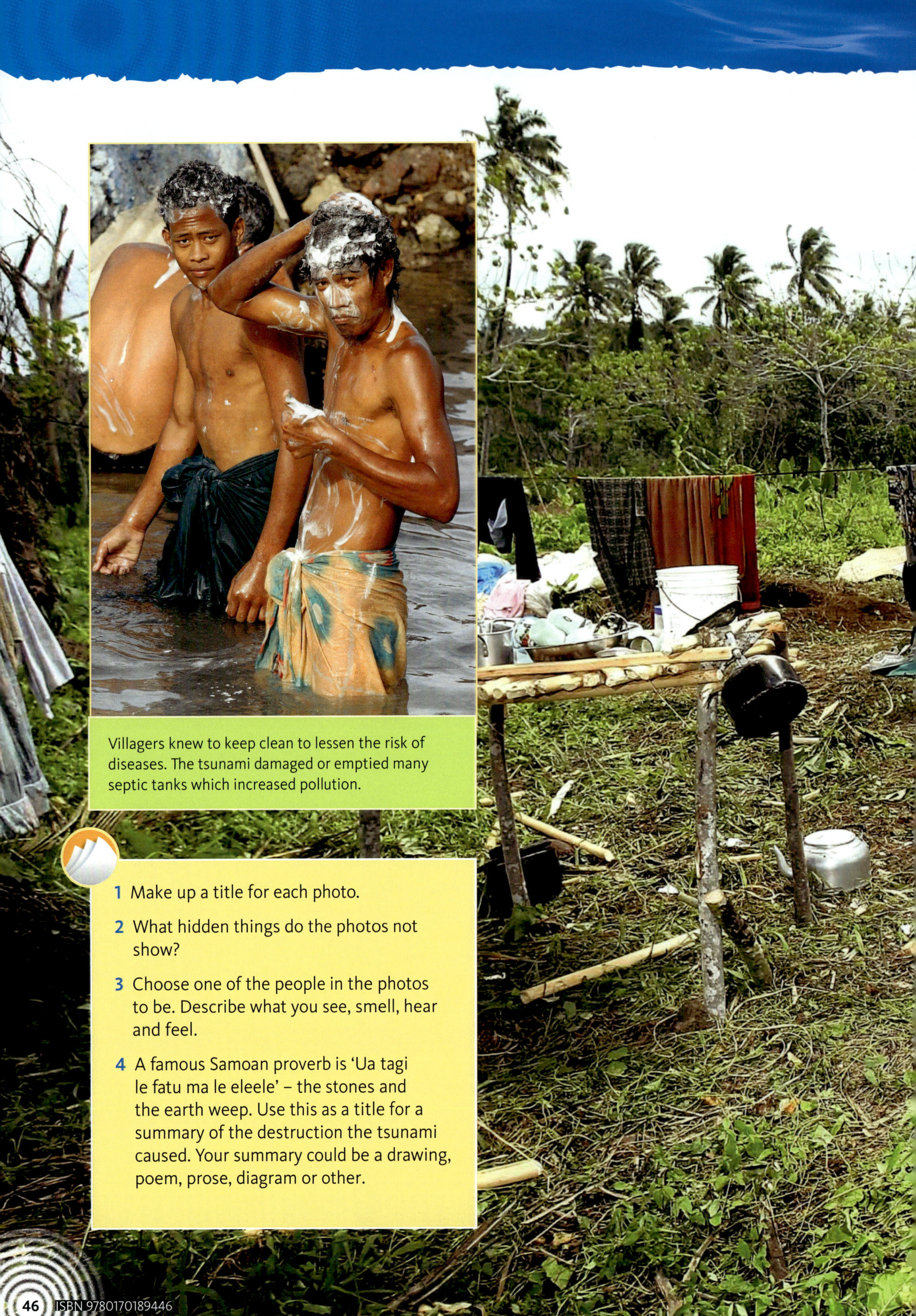

Villagers knew to keep clean to lessen the risk of diseases. The tsunami damaged or emptied many septic tanks which increased pollution.

1 Make up a title for each photo.

2 What hidden things do the photos not show?

3 Choose one of the people in the photos to be. Describe what you see, smell, hear and feel.

4 A famous Samoan proverb is 'Ua tagi le fatu ma le eleele' – the stones and the earth weep. Use this as a title for a summary of the destruction the tsunami caused. Your summary could be a drawing, poem, prose, diagram or other.

 ISBN 9780170189446

Survivors set up camp in the hills.

15 Responses to the Effects of the Tsunami

Government

The Samoan Prime Minister and Deputy Prime Minister were in New Zealand when the tsunami hit. They went home immediately. Government declared a State of Disaster. A few days later it declared a State of Emergency. This let emergency services work when and where they wanted.

Some lucky, some unlucky

Survivors realised they had escaped death. A group of Palmerston North students and teachers had kayaked the night before from Lalomanu to the island of Namua. The tsunami swept away their belongings but they got to higher ground, unlike many in Lalomanu.

Aid

Medical teams gave tetanus shots and antibiotics to survivors they found with infected wounds.

Thief

A few people took others' belongings they found in damaged areas.

Boom and thunder stopped

After the thunder and roar of the ocean everything became calmer. Many survivors were on hills. Locals were kind. One took his shirt off and gave it to a female tourist whose top was torn and bloody. Clergymen led prayers.

Hospital

Moto'otua Hospital near Apia began operations. Broken limbs and slashed bodies were common injuries. Staff were unable to cope with so many patients. Retired nurses and teachers came in to help. Trucks brought the dead in. They included a two-month-old baby and a 102-year-old woman. The hospital ran out of room for bodies. It used two large refrigerated containers. Family members visited their loved ones. They stood at the containers and cried and cried.

Who are you?

Medical experts tried to identify bodies. Because teeth are preserved they were better identifiers than fingerprints.

Ghost town

The south-east coast sheltered Apia from the tsunami. For a while, however, Apia was deserted. People stayed on higher ground. Schools and businesses closed.

Away from home

Unable or afraid to go home, thousands of villagers set up camp inland. Many began making new houses in bush they cleared. Most were too scared to go down to get medical help for injuries and chills. Mosquitoes were a problem. One group of about 50 had only two cooking pots. They made a cooking fire by rubbing flint rocks together.

Where are my relatives?

People searched for missing relatives. A fisherman who had carried and dragged his grandmother to safety came back to look for belongings. All he found was a damaged pot. He wanted to search the lagoon for his missing relatives. However, his fishing boat that he used to moor in front of his place was squashed against a house 50 metres inland.

 ISBN 9780170189446

Help on its way

The fire station just out of Apia became a distribution centre. Four-wheel-drive utes left loaded with coconuts, bananas, taro, instant noodles, tinned sardines, clothes, and cooking equipment. They drove up dirt tracks into jungle. Other aid groups took up portaloos.

Why?

People tried to understand why the disaster had happened. One suggestion was that God sent the tsunami to punish the government for forcing people to change from driving on the right side to the left.

Turtles

Villagers in the Aleipata area returned many turtles, stranded on land, to the sea. This pleased campaigners who had worked to conserve turtles.

Day of mourning

October 10 was a national day of mourning. Flags flew at half-mast all day in Apia. A memorial service took place at Apia Stadium. School children laid two white wreaths for each of the 143 casualties. They laid purple wreaths for dead foreigners.

Rescue

Some people who lived in locations such as Apia and villages along the northern coasts of Upolu and Savai'i went and brought their relatives away from the wreckage or inland camps. Public buildings housed some of those who had lost their homes.

TV

Television reporters in Samoa tried to tell the story of the tsunami but began crying. When a young boy was found buried with his school uniform on, the reporter was so upset he could not talk properly.

Prayers

On October 6 Samoans went to church. A thousand people including rescue workers crowded into the church of Lalomanu. It survived because it was located on higher ground than the destroyed beachside houses. The tsunami killed 46 people at Lalomanu.

1. What actions are associated with the following? Mourners, distributors, campaigners.
2. Why did the government declare two 'States'?
3. What does a wreath look like?
4. What does 'flags flew at half-mast' mean and why were they doing this?
5. What could happen to people who did not get medical treatment?
6. What evidence is there that Samoa is a very religious country?
7. Why would water be in short supply in damaged areas?
8. What evidence is there that the tsunami had no respect for the age of its victims?
9. Find an example of someone behaving kindly and someone behaving unkindly.
10. Why was the party from Palmerston North school lucky?

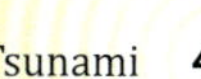

16 New Zealand Response

Individuals, groups, organisations and government in New Zealand responded to Samoa's tsunami by donating work, money, goods, friendship and time. Here are some examples.

The New Zealand Prime Minister cut short his holiday and flew to Samoa. He visited some of the most damaged areas.

A special New Zealand spotting plane searched the Samoan coast. It fired flares to show rescue boats locations of dead bodies.

A group of New Zealand-based Samoan nurses gave up their annual leave and paid their own airfares to Samoa to help local nurses.

New Zealand medical staff who flew to Samoa included nurses, doctors, a plastic surgeon, an infectious diseases specialist, grief counsellors, a psychiatrist.

The New Zealand Government gave two million dollars in emergency aid. It promised many millions more for things like housing, water, power, roads.

A New Zealand team fixed up the main pipeline along the southwest coast of Upolu. Kiwi organisations donated pipes and fittings.

New Zealand helicopters used underslung nets to drop water and food at Samoan villages.

New Zealand's Foreign Minister arrived in Samoa. He oversaw New Zealand's emergency response.

New Zealanders donated money, food, clothes, equipment.

A seven-year-old New Zealand boy set up a 'donate your pocket-money' fund for Samoa and raised hundreds of thousands of dollars.

New Zealand police technicians set up a police radio network on the southern coast of Upolu.

A group of students from King's College in South Auckland paid their own airfares to Samoa to help the clean-up.

New Zealand vets, and emergency food supplies for animals, arrived at Samoa.

New Zealand planes brought search and rescue teams to Samoa.

People in New Zealand mourned the seven New Zealanders the tsunami killed.

New Zealand paramedics went up into hills to find Samoans who needed medical help but who were too scared of another tsunami to come down for it.

New Zealand sniffer dogs were flown to Samoa. They searched for bodies in rubble and rotting vegetation. It was so hot the dogs could work for only 45 minutes at one time. The water was too hot for a swim so the dogs sheltered under palm trees. They were moved from village to village.

 ISBN 9780170189446

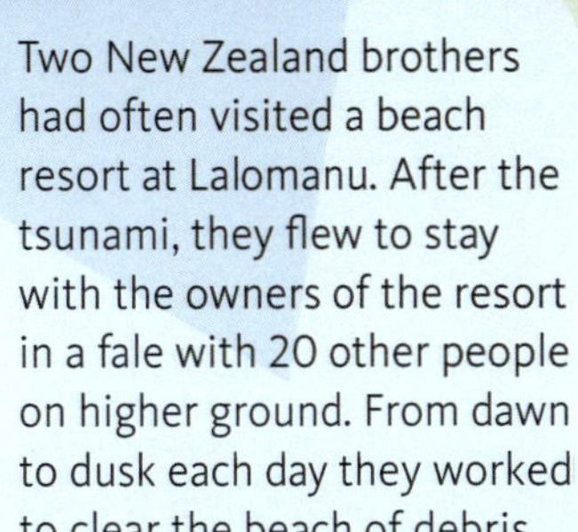

Two New Zealand brothers had often visited a beach resort at Lalomanu. After the tsunami, they flew to stay with the owners of the resort in a fale with 20 other people on higher ground. From dawn to dusk each day they worked to clear the beach of debris.

Teams of New Zealand tradespeople such as plumbers, engineers, builders, architects, drainlayers arrived to build fales and toilet blocks.

New Zealand engineers flew to Samoa and gave advice on the safety of bridges.

An elderly Samoan couple living in New Zealand donated their shared walking frame to the 84-year-old survivor who had previously used a piece of wood to help him get around.

New Zealanders donated thousands of reading glasses.

HMNZS *Canterbury* brought fale poles, telephone poles, plumbing and electrical supplies, water pipes, and aid supplies from donations.

Many New Zealand volunteers arrived in Samoa to help clean up.

New Zealand divers mended the submarine water main to Manono.

Kiwi sports stars David Tua and Inga Tuigamala flew to Samoa. The tsunami had killed one of David Tua's aunts. 'The best thing I can do for Samoa,' said Tua, 'is show my heart.'

Kings School in Auckland sent 500 desks and chairs to Samoan schools. Students added letters of friendship, t-shirts, books and pencils for Samoan students.

New Zealand police helped identify victims of the tsunami.

New Zealand planes brought to Samoa equipment such as morgues, caskets, stretchers, tents, tarpaulins, tools, chainsaws, food and a desalination plant to supply fresh water.

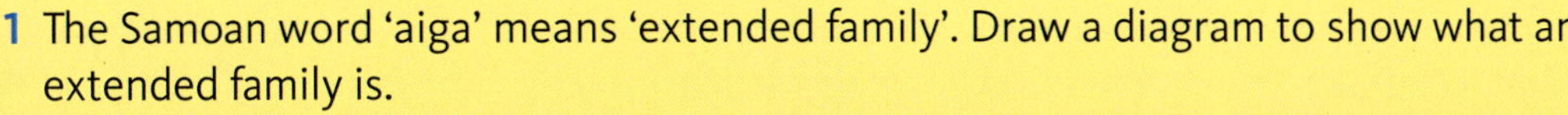

1 The Samoan word 'aiga' means 'extended family'. Draw a diagram to show what an extended family is.
2 In what ways did New Zealanders play the part of aiga after the tsunami?
3 Make a list of help that a location might need after a tsunami has hit it.
4 What did sniffer dogs do to help and how did they find working conditions?
5 What aid did New Zealand send by plane and what aid by ship?
6 How many examples can you find of New Zealanders acting in groups to help?
7 How many examples can you find of New Zealanders acting as individuals to help?

17 Long-term Effects of the Tsunami on Samoa

Samoa had a repair bill of $370 million.

Before the tsunami the Samoan Government had made a plan. To fight rising sea levels it would get villagers on the coast to shift to higher ground. Villagers may not have liked this idea. Now the tsunami had shown many the sense of the plan. In late October when authorities started to give out supplies to help people build new homes, the Prime Minister advised villagers to build homes on higher ground inland.

Tourism is important for Samoa's economy. The biggest numbers of tourists come from New Zealand. The tsunami destroyed and damaged some tourist resorts. Tourists were nervous about possible future tsunamis. Tourist organisations said New Zealanders wanting to help Samoa should keep taking their holidays there.

Before the tsunami funerals were big events. Families buried their loved ones near home. They gave money and other gifts to chiefs and others who came to the funeral. They also waited for family members overseas to return for the funeral. The tsunami meant many dead bodies lay in high temperatures. They had to be buried quickly, maybe away from their village area. There was no time to arrange for family members to come home, or to arrange big funerals. People saw that simple funerals could be fine.

Many countries and world organisations helped Samoa. For example the tsunami destroyed four primary schools and a secondary school. Students had to be relocated to host schools. UNICEF (United Nations Children's International Fund) provided tents for classrooms, School-in-a-Box kits (each providing classroom materials for about 80 students) and water tanks.

A month after the tsunami, Samoans were telling other countries that they no longer needed donations of food and clothes. What they needed was money to make roads, water pipelines and powerlines. They also wanted to finish a road they had started two years ago. It was to run along the hills behind the southern coast of Upolu.

ISBN 9780170189446

Before the tsunami officials had carried out exercises to show people what to do in a natural disaster. People learned they should go to higher ground after an earthquake or if they saw sea receding from the lagoon, even if they did not hear tsunami warnings. They learned that cars could help. However, most roads run parallel to the beach. Many people died when they got trapped inside cars in traffic jams.

When the first wall of water hit, a great-uncle lifted a two-year-old boy high in his arms and raced out the back door of the house towards the hills. The water rose and debris swirled about. With the baby still held high the man waded through to safety. Although the boy already had a name his parents changed it to honour his survival. He is now called Tsunami.

Most families rely on backyard livestock such as pigs and poultry. Some villagers keep their pigs and chickens in communal plots in inland jungle. Those animals were safe because they were located upland. But the tsunami carried off animals kept on beachfront properties in the villages on the southeast of Upolu. One man had a lucky break because he found one of his two piglets stuck in the mud, still alive. Normally animals ate leftovers. After the tsunami, there were few leftovers. People had to rethink their old attitude that animals could look after themselves.

Samoa's tourism operators wanted to rebuild on beaches. One owner whose wife drowned in the tsunami said sleeping in a house on the beach was part of the tourist package. Yet many resorts were located on beaches in front of a steep and pathless cliff. Resort owners said they would build escape routes up the cliff.

Workers cut down trees and cleared areas for people in the hills to grow food.

The tsunami carried off fishing gear, canoes, boats, goods and shops. This stopped some people earning a living.

The tsunami showed up some problems with health care. For example, doctors found that a ventilator they tried to use to save a baby did not work.

By early November medics were warning that some wounds had stopped responding to antibiotics. This could lead to gangrene and amputations. Medics also talked of Tsunami Lung, caused by high pressure polluted sea water hitting the lungs. This could lead to lung diseases.

 ISBN 9780170189446

The tsunami raised issues for future problem-solvers. For example, it had exposed an illegal rubbish dump. It had damaged the wharf at Aleipata and experts said the channel widening that had happened beforehand may have cut down on protection against the tsunami effects. The tsunami had damaged crops such as taro and breadfruit that were not high inland.

Many people suffered post traumatic stress disorder. This showed up as anxiety and depression, violence, or alcoholism. Some people were unable to sleep because they could still hear the roar of tsunami waves. It was a while before some children began to swim in the ocean again.

Coral reefs are formed by tiny animals called polyps. They provide habitats for fish and other life. The tsunami damaged some coral and dumped debris on top of reefs. Roofing iron got wrapped round the coral. However, experts said coral reefs have learned to live with tsunamis so they should recover.

1 If you were Tsunami, what would you think of your change of name?
2 What is habitat, post traumatic stress disorder, polyps, ventilator, gangrene, amputation, UNICEF, economy, School-in-a-Box kits?
3 Why were there few leftovers for animals after the tsunami?
4 Misinformation can kill. Find a piece of evidence to back this statement up.
5 Social effects are to do with people's health, education, life-style, relationships. Give the social effects of the tsunami.
6 Economic effects are to do with people's work, transport, resources. Give the economic effects of the tsunami.

18 Immediate Effect of the Tsunami on New Zealand

In New Zealand the day of the earthquake and tsunami was September 30, a Wednesday. While people arranged their day, such as students getting ready for school, scientists and organisations were having to deal with a possible tsunami hitting New Zealand. Luckily, there was enough time to warn people.

The warning in New Zealand

Member countries of the Pacific Tsunami Warning Center in Hawaii sent it data, as usual, on seismic activity. Because the earthquake was bigger than 7.5 magnitude, the Center issued a tsunami alert and warning for the Pacific. It sent an email message to New Zealand's Ministry of Civil Defence and Emergency Management in Wellington. It put the quake's magnitude at 8.3 and recorded a 78 mm rise in sea levels near the epicentre. It issued a general alert for the South Pacific region from American Samoa to New Zealand. It issued a tsunami warning for many islands in the Pacific including the Samoas, the Cook Islands, Tonga, Fiji, New Zealand. It put out a tsunami watch for other locations such as Hawaii, Vanuatu, Papua New Guinea and New Caledonia.

Note the American spelling of **Center**.

In Wellington staff at GNS Science (Institute of Geological and Nuclear Sciences Ltd) analysed their data and began sending information to the Ministry of Civil Defence and Emergency Management.

The Ministry analysed all the information and sent out tsunami alerts to regional authorities, the police, the Defence Force and local emergency organisations. Those groups can send warnings to the public by radio, television, phones. People registered on the system of some local councils get an automated phone call warning.

The PTWC aims to:

- find and locate big earthquakes in the Pacific region.
- see if the earthquake has generated a tsunami.
- give tsunami information and warnings to people to lessen the hazards of tsunamis, especially to humans.

To do this it:

- continuously monitors seismic activity and sea level at sites in the Pacific run by member countries.
- has a team of tsunami specialists who live on site so the duty person can get to a desk at the Center within minutes and issue the first earthquake information within ten to 20 minutes.

This was the time-line for the warnings in New Zealand.

6.48 am	7.04	7.35	8.43	9.58
Earthquake off Samoa.	Pacific Tsunami Warning Center sent warning email to Wellington.	National warning put out: 'There is a threat of a damaging tsunami impacting on the New Zealand coastline. The tsunami warning will remain in effect until a cancellation message is issued by the Ministry of Civil Defence ...'	Warning estimated wave heights at 1m at the East Coast and Bay of Plenty.	Warning confirmed 1m estimate. Specific warning for beach areas and small boats.

 ISBN 9780170189446

Radio and television told people about the tsunami and kept updating them throughout the day. Local authorities put out warnings such as:

- People in low-lying areas of the Coromandel coast were advised to move to higher ground immediately. Fire service staff drove round urging them to move.
- Environment Waikato told harbourmasters not to move on the water. Waikato Civil Defence said people living or working on coasts should be on high alert.
- Hawke's Bay Civil Defence told people to keep away from beaches. People in Te Kaha on the East Cape were told to go to high ground.
- Auckland regional authorities advised people on Great Barrier Island, Waiheke Island and on regional coastlines to go to higher ground.
- A helicopter flew along the Bay of Plenty coast and through a loudhailer advised people to keep away from the beach.

The warnings were specific. For example, the tsunami was predicted to hit East Cape at 9.44am, Gisborne at 10.00, Napier at 10.40, Wellington at 10.50, Auckland at 11.12. Even so, some people went to the coastline to look for the tsunami. Some did climb hills to watch but the hills were close to the beach. Many at Mount Maunganui and Gisborne ignored the warnings. Although Kiwifruit marketer Zespri evacuated its office in Mount Maunganui, some families with small children kept playing in the sand. Tauranga police finally cleared the Mount's main beach when it got the last surfers out of the water.

New Zealand sea level gauges (Samoa tsunami)

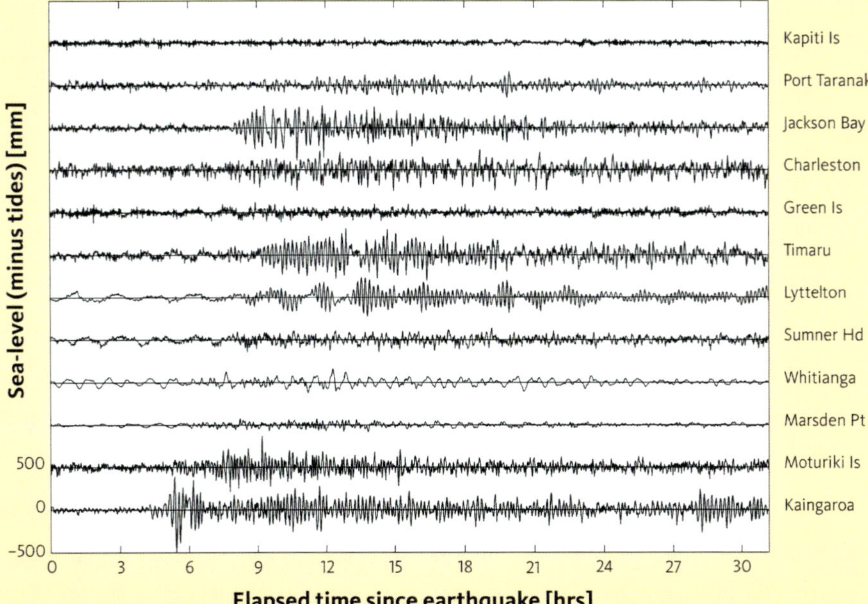

elapsed	gone, passed by
hrs	hours
gauge	measuring instrument
sea level gauge	instrument for measuring sea level and therefore possible tsunami
Hd	Head
Pt	Point
Is	Island
mm	millimetre (one thousandth of a metre)
0	'normal' sea level
500	500mm above 0
-500	500mm below 0

0.25	11.11	12.16pm	13.25	16.10
Warning downgraded o national advisory nformation and/or advice).	Advisory put out saying that although Pacific Tsunami Warning Center had cancelled its warning for New Zealand, a wave reading at Raoul Island suggested a second, bigger wave was on its way, possibly arriving at 11.15 am. It said there may be further waves.	Advisory of further waves possible for the next hour.	Advisory of more waves and strong currents.	Advisory cancelled. Mention again of strong currents. Final media release.

When the tsunami failed to send spectacular waves, some people were disappointed. Yet the tsunami did arrive, despite New Zealand being over 2,800 kms away from the Samoa area. It was recorded along the whole east coast of New Zealand and on most of the west coast. The biggest wave was at the Chathams. It was nearly 0.9 m from crest to trough. The tsunami arrived at various times. For example, it arrived at the Chathams 4.2 hours after the earthquake. It arrived in Westland about 8 hours after the earthquake. The peak wave at the Chathams came more than an hour after the first tsunami wave there. Peak waves at Christchurch and Taranaki did not arrive until about 12-13 hours after the first tsunami waves.

1 What do you do when you 'analyse data'?
2 What is the name of the Ministry that deals with natural disasters?
3 Which New Zealand organisation sends information to the Ministry?
4 Would you like to work in the PTWC? Give a reason for your answer.
5 Why is the PTWC important to New Zealand?
6 How has the cartoonist shown action in the cartoon on page 57?
7 What comment about the behaviour of some people is that cartoonist making?
8 How has the cartoonist shown action in the cartoon on page 58?
9 What comment about the behaviour of some people is that cartoonist making?
10 Find an example of sensible behaviour during the 2009 tsunami warning and find an example of not-so-sensible behaviour.
11 Give five things about the New Zealand sea level gauges graph on page 57. They can be features of a graph or information that the graph shows.

 ISBN 9780170189446

19 Does New Zealand really get Tsunamis?

The tsunami warning made people in New Zealand think. Many asked, *Do we really get tsunamis here?*

The answer is YES.

New Zealand was lucky on 30 September 2009 because the tsunami from the Samoa earthquake caused no major damage. Other tsunamis in the past had done much more damage.

Tsunamis before written records of events ...

- are called paleotsunamis.
- have deposited sediment and debris at many locations around the New Zealand coast.
- include one from a meteor impact because scientists have found a big meteor crater south west of Stewart Island and say the impact would have generated a tsunami more than 50 metres high.
- possibly caused many Maori to shift from coastal locations to hilltops in the middle of the 15th century. Some of their old coastal locations show evidence of tsunami flooding and Maori oral tradition records tsunamis that killed many people.

sediment = material such as sand, silt, plant remains

Tsunami since written records

Distance-source tsunamis

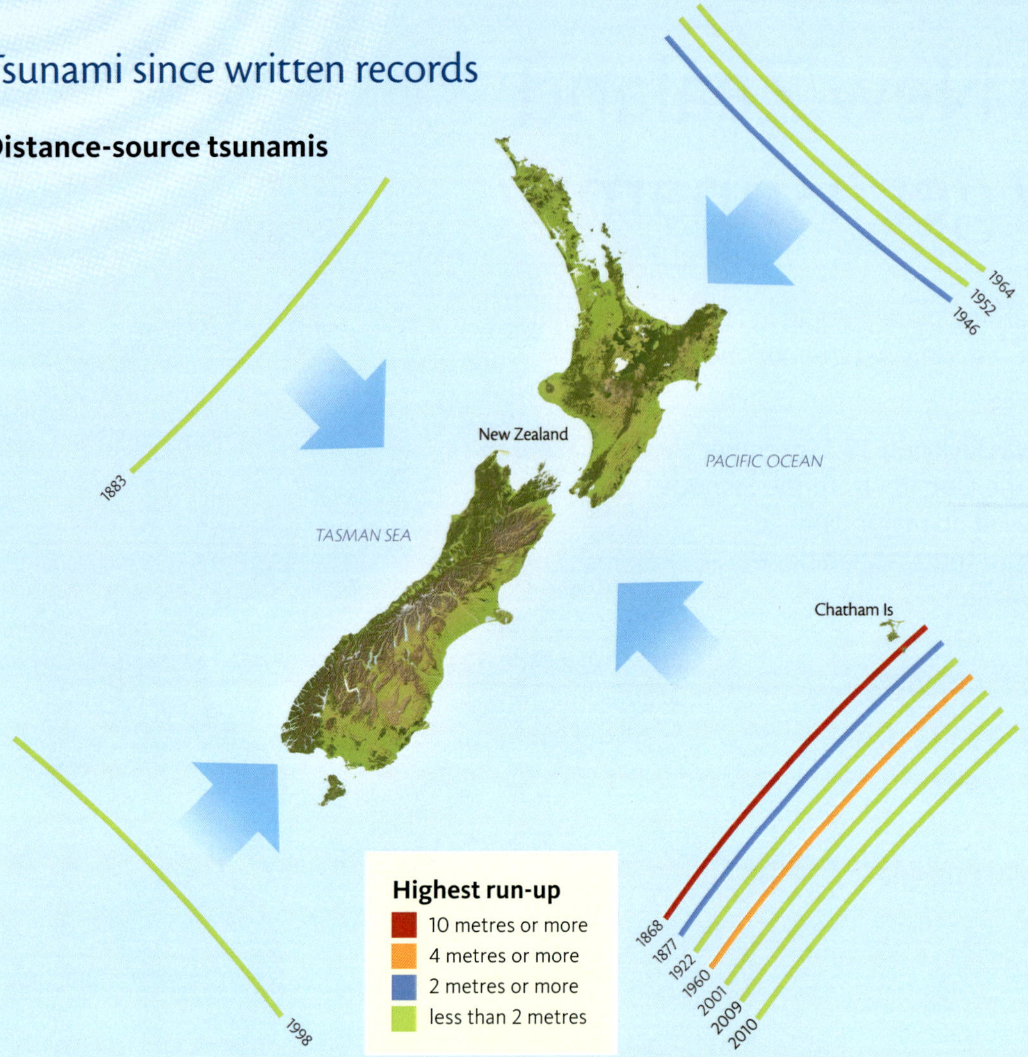

1964
1952
1946
1883
New Zealand
PACIFIC OCEAN
TASMAN SEA
Chatham Is
1998
Highest run-up
10 metres or more
4 metres or more
2 metres or more
less than 2 metres
1868
1877
1922
1960
2001
2009
2010

1855 Tsunami

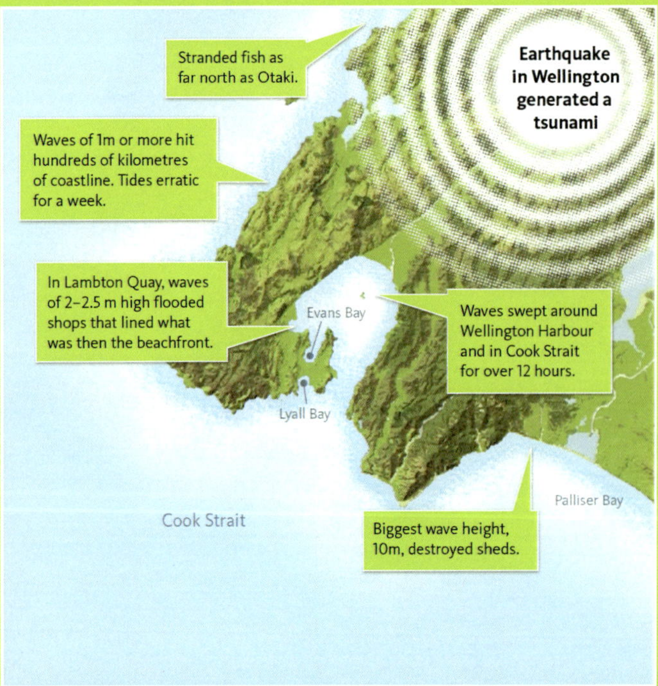

Stranded fish as far north as Otaki.
Earthquake in Wellington generated a tsunami
Waves of 1m or more hit hundreds of kilometres of coastline. Tides erratic for a week.
In Lambton Quay, waves of 2–2.5 m high flooded shops that lined what was then the beachfront.
Evans Bay
Waves swept around Wellington Harbour and in Cook Strait for over 12 hours.
Lyall Bay
Cook Strait
Palliser Bay
Biggest wave height, 10m, destroyed sheds.

1868 Tsunami

Water drained from Lyttelton harbour, left ships sitting on mud. Then waves rose by over 7m. Ships smashed into wharves and each other. Further big waves arrived over several hours. For days water levels were erratic. Floods along valleys in bays damaged houses, swept away bridges and fences.
Water roared into houses in a Maori village and woke people. They fled to higher ground. Two more waves, of up to 10m high, destroyed village and some European houses. Water swept a Maori out to sea and drowned him. It smashed wagons, shifted heavy stones.
Several hours later
15 hours
Earthquake in South America generated a tsunami
Banks Peninsula
in New Zealand
Chatham Islands
(Part of New Zealand)

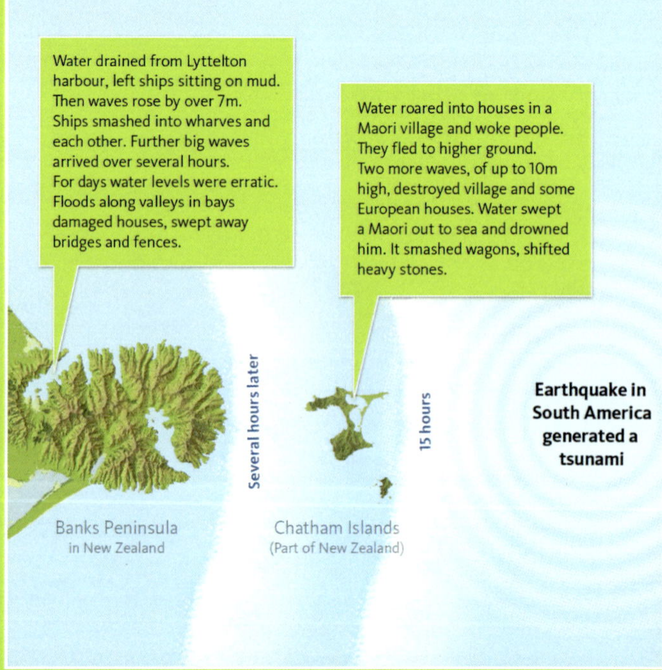

 ISBN 9780170189446

1 Look at the distant-source tsunamis map and answer the following.
   a What do the dates represent?
   b Name features that make this map on page 60 a good map.
   c What would the term 'run-up' mean?
   d From which direction have the majority of tsunamis come?
   e In what year was the biggest tsunami?
   f What paletsunamis would have been bigger than those shown on the map?
   g Why are there no tsunamis shown in the mid 15th century?

2 Make up a title for each photo.

The 1960 tsunami flooded Gisborne Harbour.

These people have gone to higher ground several days after the 1960 tsunami when a radio message warned of another possible tsunami.

The 1947 tsunami on the coast north of Gisborne stranded fish.

3 Which of the four examples (below) of tsunamis since written records would you use if you were writing about tsunamis and needed an example? Give reasons for your choice.

1947 Tsunami

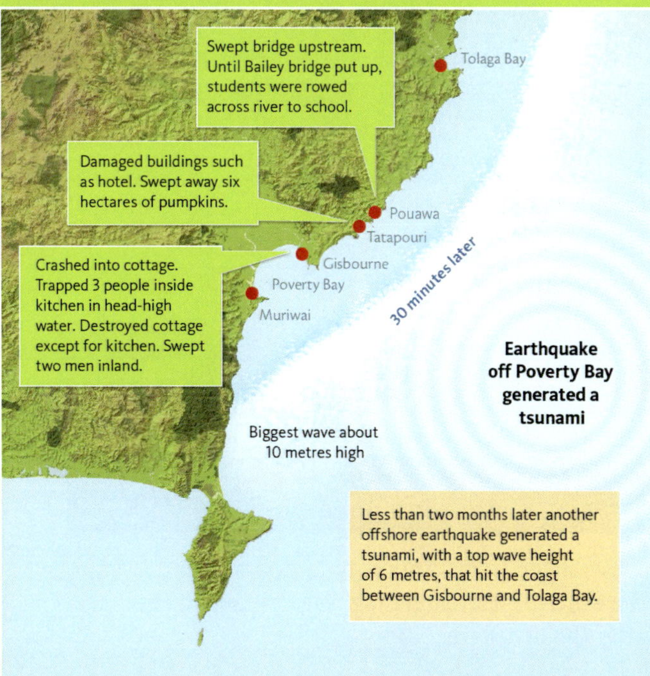

1960 Tsunami

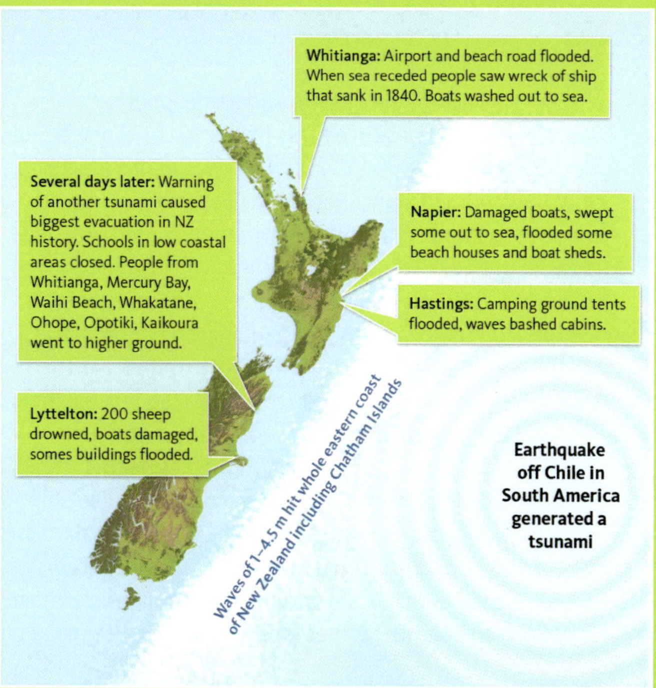

20 2010 Tsunami from Chile

If an earthquake close to New Zealand generates a local-source tsunami, the first waves can reach the coast within minutes. But if an earthquake way over on the South American coast, say off Chile, generates a distant-source tsunami, the waves will have to travel at least 9,300 kilometres before they reach New Zealand. This will take them many hours.

Waves from distant-source tsunami can take a while to build up to a peak wave height. So it can be a few hours later after the first wave before the highest wave appears. It is usually not straight from the source area. When waves move onto a continental shelf, which is the shallower shelf of sea around a land mass, they can grow in height. They then start a process in certain harbours and parts of the coast such as Lyttelton Harbour, Pegasus Bay, and Whitianga of sloshing back and forth. So a peak wave height can take a few hours to build up. Waves can also reflect backwards and forwards off headlands, underwater ridges such as Chatham Rise, and neighbouring countries such as Australia. They may eventually join up to form higher waves in some locations. These waves can get trapped in shallow water when they are near the shore, and then they start moving along the coast and can build up in height due to friction effects from the seabed.

Example

On 27 February 2010 an earthquake of 8.8 on the moment magnitude scale occurred at a depth of 35 km 115 km NNE off the Chilean city of Concepcion. The quake, one of the biggest recorded, was so strong it possibly shifted Earth's axis and shortened the day.

The earthquake and the tsunami it generated killed hundreds of people in Chile.

Tsunami warnings went out for the Pacific. Hundreds of thousands of people in Japan evacuated. Thousands in Samoa, Fiji, Tonga, Tuvalu, the Cook Islands and Hawaii moved up to higher ground.

NOAA (US National Oceanic and Atmospheric Administration) produced this image to show projected (estimated) times that the tsunami would hit other locations in the Pacific. People in Gisborne and Napier were evacuated from coastal homes and camp grounds. People in Banks Peninsula were told to stay ready to evacuate. Officials cancelled many coastal events such as the Dragonboat festival in Wellington Harbour and a half-marathon in Auckland. The Tory Channel in the Marlborough Sounds closed which delayed interislander ferries. The port of Napier closed. Ships in port were taken out into water of at least 30 metres deep. Other vessels, due in port, waited off the coast. A cruise ship cancelled its visit. Waves reached the Chatham Islands about 11.6 hours after the earthquake. They reached the North Island, at East Cape, nearly an hour later. At most locations the highest waves were not the first to arrive.

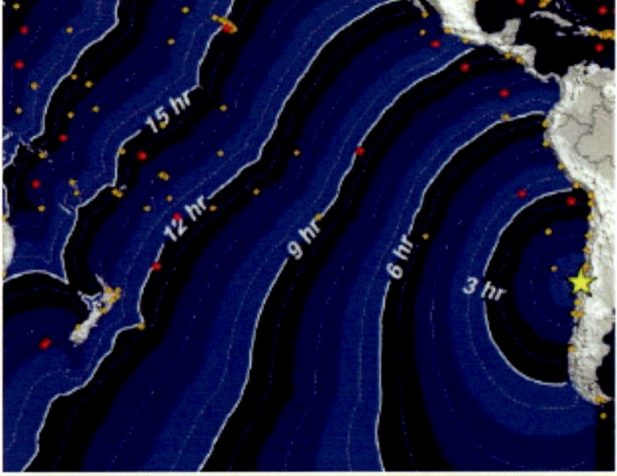

They ranged from 1.2 hours to 26 hours after the first wave arrived. Lyttelton's highest wave was six hours after the first wave.

 ISBN 9780170189446

NOAA also produced this image to show projected wave heights. It shows that by the time the tsunami would hit New Zealand the waves would be much smaller than those that hit Chile. The waves that arrived first, at Scott Base in the Ross Sea (Antarctica), were small. Lyttelton had the largest waves. The highest wave of 1.9 metres came in mid-afternoon. Other peak wave heights over a metre were measured in Chatham Islands, Gisborne, Christchurch, Timaru and Whitianga. The tsunami was measured all along the west coast as well, but top wave heights were 0.3–0.5 metres. At each location, the first wave was an upwards rise rather than a drawback of the water level. The biggest disturbance was at Tutukaka, east of Whangarei. The water surged in and out all morning in churning and sucking movements that looked like a huge boiling saucepan. Boats from Tutukaka Harbour went out to sea to avoid the surges. Like the rest of Northland, residents were warned to stay away from beaches.

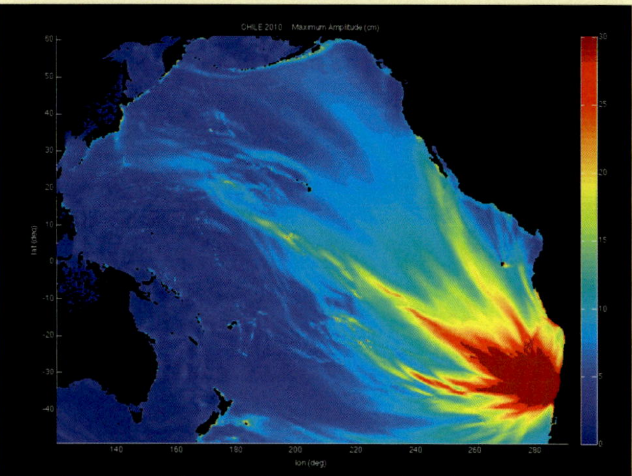

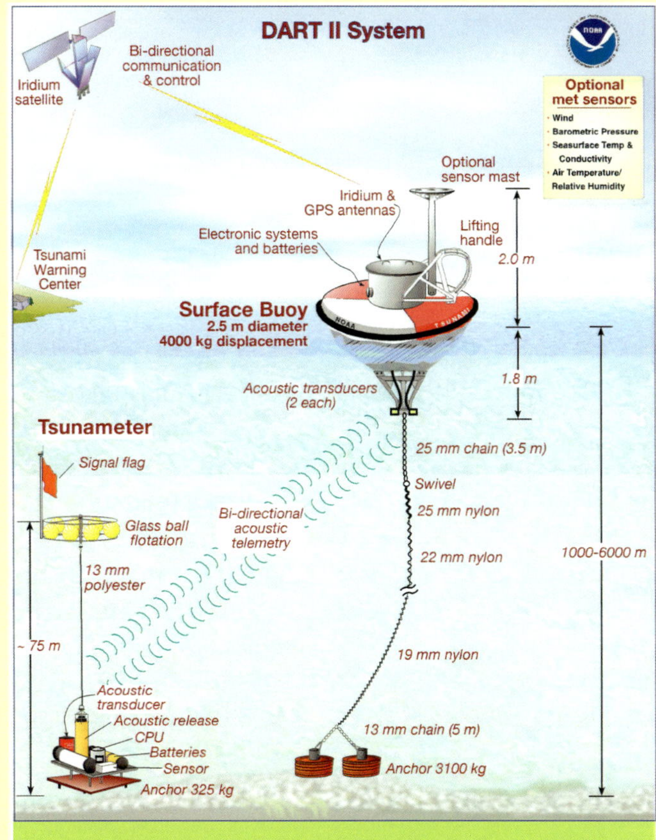

This is a DART buoy used to detect tsunamis. DART stands for Deep-ocean Assessment and Reporting of Tsunamis.

1 In what ways can waves from a distant-source tsunami be different to waves from a local-source tsunami?

2 With a partner or group, make a globe with the outline of the continents on it. Mark in the source of the February 2010 tsunami. Mark in New Zealand. Draw a thick line from the source to Tutukaka. In no more than two sentences, describe the amount of space on Earth occupied by the Pacific, and the distance and effect on New Zealand of the tsunami.

3 Describe how a DART buoy works.

4 Look at the map of wave heights. What do the colours represent, what colours are closest to New Zealand, and what do they show about the possible impact of the tsunami?

5 Look at the map of wave times. What do the red diamonds represent?

6 According to the map, about how long would New Zealand have to wait for the first waves to hit the mainland? How accurate did this forecast turn out to be?

21 Can Humans Protect Themselves from Tsunamis?

A human response to a tsunami is to work out ways to protect themselves from ones in the future. The effect of a tsunami depends on where and when it hits.

For example

1 The 2009 tsunami hit Samoa's southern coast. This was where many resorts and villages were so impact was very high.

2 New Zealand's past big tsunamis struck when fewer people lived along the coast. Today there is a much bigger population and cultural environment there so tsunami impact would be higher.

3 Big earthquakes happen on the boundary between the Pacific and South American plates. Therefore the west coast of South America is a source of many tsunamis in the Pacific. These will hit New Zealand's east coasts. However, tsunamis do spread around the land and through Cook Strait. Therefore the west coast may get big waves.

Some things humans can do to lessen the effects of tsunamis

1 Use warning systems for distance-source tsunamis

Travel times of the tsunami from the 1960 Chilean earthquake.

Scientists can work out arrival times for a distant-source tsunami, sometimes called a teletsunami. They use water depths, time of the event that generated the tsunami, and distance from the event. This gives time to warn the public.

 ISBN 9780170189446

Sea gauges are useful for distant-source tsunamis. Although Samoa had a seismic gauge at the Apia wharf it was no use in the 2009 tsunami. New Zealand has a network of gauges around the country. Inside the gauge are sensors. They measure the height of the water column above them. Instruments in the network send data by radio to GNS Science. Although not all gauges planned for New Zealand's network were installed at the time of the 2009 tsunami, some gauges picked up the tsunami as it neared the New Zealand coast. Some gauges recorded differences in sea levels of up to a metre. Some showed unusual sea surface up to almost 30 hours after the earthquake. The tsunami arrived at the two Raoul Island locations first, followed by North Cape, East Cape, Chatham Island, Gisborne and Napier.

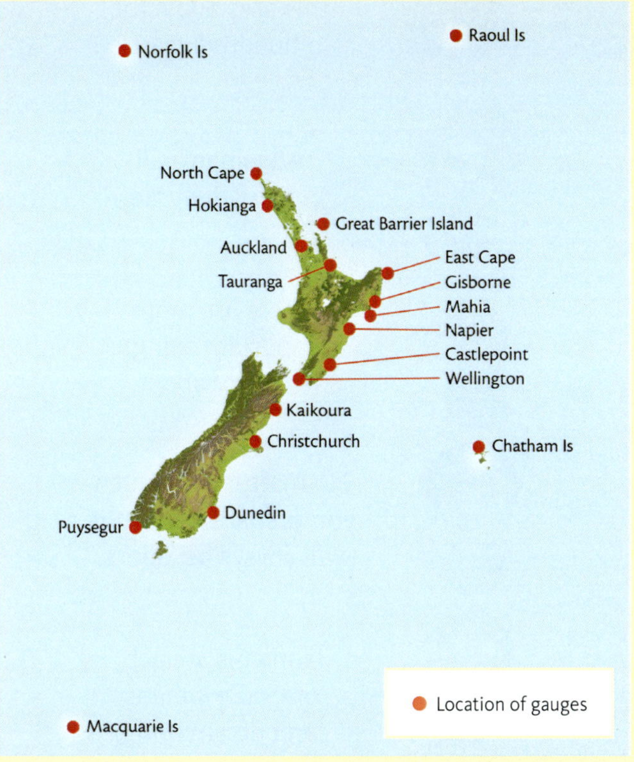

2 Make warning systems for local-source tsunamis

Japan is the only country with a warning system for a local-source tsunami. It has an automatic earthquake location system. The system is based on hundreds of seismographs. Japanese scientists have worked out what tsunamis could come from 100,000 different earthquakes at 10,000 locations around the Japanese coast.

3 Engineering

Japan, for example, has built some seawalls. People say these block sea views, reduce public access to beaches, and can topple over or break up. They can make people think they are safe from tsunamis and therefore people stop being prepared for one.

Japanese seawall.

4 Change people's minds

A tsunami won't hit this area again for a hundred years.

Another tsunami could hit today, or tomorrow.

A tsumani will never affect me.

You never know where you might end up living or on holiday.

There are more important things to worry about.

The idea is not to worry about tsunamis, just be prepared.

No matter how much you prepare, tsunamis will always be killers.

History shows that being prepared will help me survive.

Tsunamis are acts of God. Humans can't do anything.

Humans are not powerless; they can do heaps.

Tsunamis are so strong it's pointless trying to lessen the risk.

Not all tsunamis are towering ten metre waves.

Someone will be there to help me.

Someone may or may not be there to help me.

5 Have a disaster plan

This helps the human response to be automatic. For example, the staff at the Museum of New Zealand Te Papa Tongarewa in Wellington would move everyone up to the top floors if a tsunami struck.

 ISBN 9780170189446

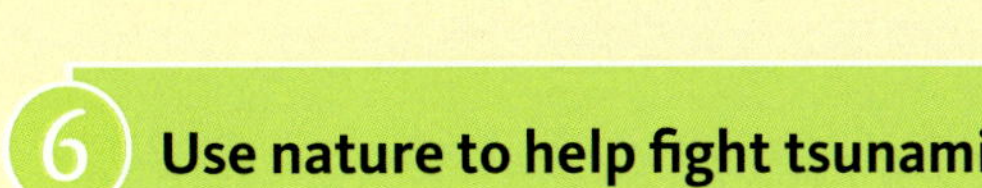

6 Use nature to help fight tsunamis

Tsunamis can travel several kilometres inland. Setting rules for how close people can build to the coast won't necessarily protect people. However, green belts, dunes, mangroves and replanting with native vegetation can reduce the impact of a tsunami by absorbing a lot of its energy.

7 Follow advice

Before the tsunami

- Keep a radio or television on all the time.
- Don't leave your house unless authorities tell you to and then do so immediately.
- If you leave, take essential items such as your asthma medication.
- Stay off beaches and off the water until authorities cancel the warning.
- If you are on a boat stay in the water and don't return to port until authorities cancel the warning.

During the tsunami

- Don't try to save any possessions.
- If you are trapped under or in water, stay calm. Panic will make things worse.
- Grab hold of something that floats to help you stay above the water.
- Look for a chance to let go of the floating debris and climb on to something high out of the water.
- Don't climb a tree unless that's your only choice. Water can uproot or smash it. If you must climb, go as high as you can.

After the tsunami

- Check yourself for injuries and get help if necessary.
- If someone needs to be rescued, get experts with the right gear. Acting on your own might get yourself killed or injured.
- Give help to people who need it most such as children, elderly, carless, people with disabilities.
- Keep listening for updated emergency information.
- Avoid disaster areas. You will be in the way of rescue teams and at risk from things like polluted water or crumpled roads.

1 Look at the map of New Zealand's gauges (page 65) and answer the following.
   a Which is the nearest gauge to where you live?
   b There are 20 gauges in the New Zealand network. Yet the map shows only 19 locations. Why is this?
   c On which coast are the majority of gauges located? Why?
2 Look at the map of Travel Times (page 64) and answer the following.
   a What do the figures represent?
   b How long did the tsunami take to get to New Zealand?
   c Would you expect Chile to suffer many deaths in the 1960 tsunami? Give a reason for your answer.
3 Make up a set of five questions (called a questionnaire) that you could ask people to see how tsunami-aware they are.
4 'There is no single measure that can provide complete protection.' Give your opinions for or against this comment.
5 The photo below was taken in Hilo, Hawaii, during the 1946 tsunami. Locate the tsunami in the photo and decide if the young men would have been safe or not.
6 Give a reason for the following.
   a You should avoid rushing to places where a tsunami has just hit.
   b If you are on a boat during a tsunami warning you should not return to port.
   c House-owners on the beach-front are encouraged to replace lawns on dunes with native vegetation.
   d The west coast of South America is the source of many tsunamis.
   e It takes a lot of work to make a warning system for a local-source tsunami.
   f Tsunami impact today is likely to be higher in New Zealand than a hundred years ago.
7 The policeman in the photo below was on duty during a tsunami alert for New Zealand. With a partner, prepare some dialogue (speaking) that could be taking place.

 ISBN 9780170189446

22 Tofa – Goodbye

Samoa's Report Card for the beginning of 2010

Donated aid: From many countries, especially New Zealand and Australia who were continuing to supply it.

Loan: $9.3 million from International Monetary Fund.

Housing: Money and materials available to rebuild the thousands of homes the tsunami had destroyed. Some families had moved inland and rebuilt their houses there. Many villagers were still in temporary shelters in hill plantations behind old village locations by lagoons.

Coastal debris: Some areas cleared; some still needed clearing.

Roads: New ones being built; damaged ones being rebuilt.

Powerlines: Going in along roads heading to new inland settlements.

Fresh water supplies: Water pipes to follow powerlines.

Tourism: Government was saying how important it was to help the tourist industry. Resorts being rebuilt. Government campaign called 'It's Still Beautiful' aimed to encourage tourists to visit.

Medical: Hospital still treating patients from tsunami.

Agriculture: Organisations such as Oxfam helping with schemes such as organic vegetable and fruit production.

Economy: Experts said the tsunami will make it harder to recover from the global down-turn.

Hearts and minds: Samoans said they had started to heal although they still mourned lost family and friends. Their spirit was strong.

Tofa – goodbye.

1 The 1960 Chilean earthquake had sent tsunami waves sweeping up east Upolu and the 1981 South American earthquake had sent tsunami waves inland at Manono Island and at Taga on Savai'i. It was the 2009 tsunami, however, that captured the attention of the world. Suggest some reasons why.

2 Write a summary of about five lines of the Samoan report card.

3 Check out the cartoon and answer the following.
- **a** What is the name of the cartoonist?
- **b** How has he suggested the setting of the cartoon is Samoa?
- **c** What has happened to the environment and why?
- **d** What is the central image in the cartoon and what does it represent?
- **e** Draw your own cartoon of the same location today.

4 With a partner or a group prepare something about tsunamis to share with the class.

23 How to Answer Test/Exam Questions

Paragragh writing

A paragraph is a group of sentences about one particular topic. The sentences are arranged on the page so they follow one another with no breaks between them. The next paragraph starts on a new line even when there is a lot of space left on the previous line.

One recipe for how to write a paragraph is the **GEED** recipe.

Step 1 **G = G**eneralisation – a general statement at the beginning of the paragraph saying what the topic is about.

Step 2 **E = E**xplanation – explaining the generalisation and giving more information about it.

Step 3 **E = E**xample, or Elaboration – giving examples or elaboration (further details) to support the generalisation.

Step 4 **D = D**iagram (or drawing, or photo or any other graphic to do with the topic). This is optional.

You may be asked to write a paragraph to demonstrate your communication skills and your understanding of the topic. You will need to show:

- **you have read the question properly.** (If the question asks you to explain how processes generated a tsunami you must write about the series of actions that generated a tsunami and not about how you went to Samoa six months after the tsunami there.)
- **you have learnt about and understood the topic.** (Instead of just saying vaguely that a tsunami is a series of big waves, you must explain that its generation involves a sequence of related processes and then explain what the processes are.)
- **you know how to write your knowledge in a paragraph that is clear and easy for the reader to follow and understand.** (You write a sentence that explains what a process is and another sentence that explains how a tsunami is generated by natural processes. Then you write sentences explaining what the processes are. You might choose to include a sketch of the processes involved.)

Example

Processes are the actions that shape environments. The generation of the Samoan tsunami was a series of natural processes. The first process involved Earth's tectonic plates. A break in the Pacific Plate as it went into a trench beneath the Indo-Australian Plate caused an earthquake of 8.3 magnitude. The next process was the movement of the ocean floor displacing a large amount of water ...

 ISBN 9780170189446

For example, here is a paragraph answer on 'Why the response to the Samoa tsunami did not include refugee camps'.

Step 1
The first two sentences are the generalisation as they are general statements at the beginning saying what the topic is about.

Step 2
The generalisation says refugee camps were unnecessary because of how society is organised. These five sentences explain the generalisation by giving two ways society is organised – population and aiga.

Step 3
The last two sentences elaborate on the generalisation and explanation by giving further details.

Step 4
A sketch map of Upolu, the main island affected, shows you know where Apia is, which coast the tsunami damaged and where the hills are that still house survivors.

Often a response to a natural disaster is the setting up of refugee camps to house people who have lost, or been forced to flee from, their homes. Although the tsunami wiped out many villages on the southern coast of Samoa, especially in Upolu, and sent survivors fleeing inland, refugee camps were unnecessary because of how society is organised. Samoa has a population measured in thousands rather than millions. No area is densely populated, even along the picturesque southern coasts. This meant there was not a huge number needing emergency shelter. Some survivors who did need it were taken from the disaster area by aiga who lived in unaffected areas such as Apia. Others were able to move up into the mountains and hills because the coastal villages own land there. All that is necessary for any villager to use the land for cultivation or shelter is permission from a matai. Even today, many survivors remain up there but they are on village land and not in refugee camps.

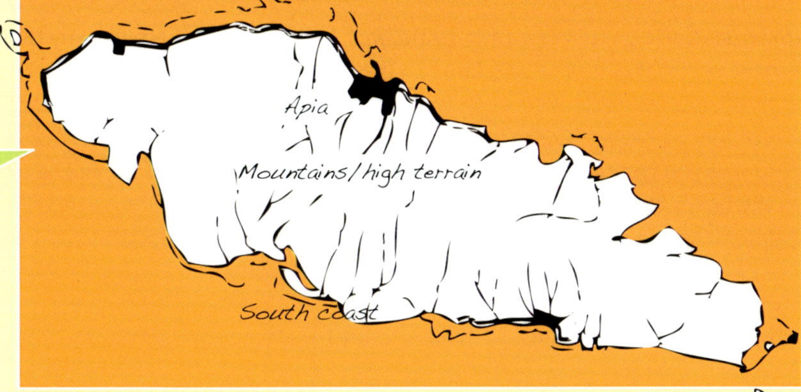

Choose one of the following topics to practise writing a paragraph.

- **a** The term tsunami was created by fishermen who returned from sea to find the harbour area destroyed. How accurate is the term tsunami?
- **b** One factor (thing) that helps decide the effects of a tsunami on a particular location is whether it is a local tsunami or not. What other factors help decide the effects of a tsunami?
- **c** Why and how do most earthquakes happen around plate boundaries?
- **d** Why did the 2009 earthquake near Samoa generate a tsunami?
- **e** Describe some things humans can do to lessen the effects of a tsunami.
- **f** Explain why the 2009 tsunami killed people in Samoa but not in New Zealand.

Resource study

A resource is information on a particular topic. It could be a map of the Ring of Fire. It could be a time line of big tsunami around the world. It could be a cartoon about people rushing to a beach to see a tsunami. You may be asked to study or check out or look carefully at a resource and then answer some questions about the resource. You will need to show:

- **you have studied the resource carefully and understood it.** (Eg. Your answers should refer to information in the resource and not something else such as a movie you saw about a tsunami.)
- **you understand the information in the resource.** (Eg. A graph uses abbreviations and you should know, or be able to work out, things such as EQ stands for earthquake.)
- **you can use skills such as thinking, using words and symbols, and problem-solving.** (Eg. You should analyse the resource to find the answer to a question such as 'What number event, in the tsunami process shown in the drawing, is the receding of the ocean?')
- **you can present your answers clearly.** (Eg. How do you think a marker would feel when you write the word 'tsunami' as 'tsumina', not once but six times in your answers?)

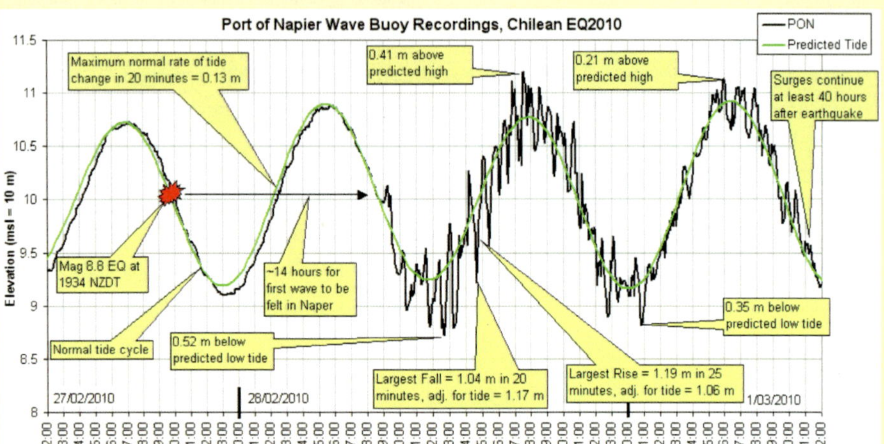

Some questions on this resource could be:

1. **Explain what the resource is about.** (The title is a good place to start – Port of Napier Wave Buoy Recordings, Chilean EQ2010. From the layout of the resource you can see it is a graph. The information in the boxes talks about the first wave to be felt in Napier, and the rise and fall and surges, which shows it is a graph of the effects of the tsunami which followed the earthquake.)
2. **What does the red explosion symbol refer to?** (This is shown in the box that has the arrow pointing to the red symbol. It says 'Mag 8.8 EQ ..'. This stands for 'Magnitude 8.8 earthquake, which shows you that the red symbol will be the earthquake.)
3. **What does '1934 NZDT' mean?** (NZDT = New Zealand Daylight Time. The earthquake happened at 3.34 local Chile time; on the 24-hour clock it was 7.34 in New Zealand. You could work that out by looking at the numbers along the bottom of the graph and seeing that the red symbol is between 19:00 and 20:00.)
4. **Give the four words on the graph used for the movement of tsunami water.** ('Tsunami water' means you must ignore 'normal tide' and so the words would be wave, fall, rise, surges.)
5. **How many hours after the earthquake was the first wave felt in Napier and how is this shown on the graph?** (There is a box with its arrow pointing to a line that runs from the earthquake symbol towards the time of the first wave, and the box says it is ~14 hours for the first wave to be felt in Napier. The symbol ~ here stands for about, or roughly similar. In addition, the arrow points to where the first spike on the Port of Napier line takes place which is on the 9:00 line and that is roughly similar to 14 hours after 19.34. Those are the two ways the graph tells you the answer is 'About 14 hours.')
6. **Describe movement on the PON line.** (PON = Port of Napier. Its line is fairly smooth until 9:00 when it suddenly begins to spike. This spiking moves the line above and below the Predicted Tide line as it traces the effect of the tsunami water.)
7. **What does the abbreviation 'adj.' mean?** (It is used in the two boxes describing the largest rise and fall. The boxes firstly say '1.04 m in 20 minutes and 1.19 m in 25 minutes. The boxes then say 'adj. for tide' and give two different measurements. This shows you the measurements have been changed or adjusted to take into account the tide. Therefore the answer is 'Adj. stands for 'adjusted'.)

 ISBN 9780170189446